Pentecostal Mission Strategies for Japan

Belong, Experience, Believe: Pentecostal Mission Strategies for Japan

Noriyuki Miyake

Printed and bound in Great Britain by Lightning Source,
Milton Keynes

Acknowledgments

With deep gratitude to God for the lives of the faithful people without whose assistance this study would not have been possible:

- My mentor Dr. Julie Ma, with great respect to her for her patient and untiring efforts in guiding and enabling me over and beyond the call of duty to finish this thesis.

- My dear parents Rev. and Mrs. Miyake, for their support and to whom I owe what I am today.

- My faithful and patient wife Chikako and our wonderful children Eimi and Lena, for sacrificing many hours of family time and for standing behind me in this endeavour, several times asking me in the final stages, "Are you done?"

- My beloved congregation of Grace Gospel Christ Church in Tokyo, Japan, for their eager prayer for this work.

And thanks to God for the needed patience, for physical and mental energy, and for spiritual refreshing during the years of the study. All glory and praise be to our Lord Jesus Christ for whose kingdom this work is done.

Dedicated

To the Lord's glory and the expansion of His Kingdom on this Earth among Japanese people.

To my parents.

To Chikako, my dear, patient wife, and to Eimi and Lena, our two beautiful children.

Contents

Chapter 1

Introduction

Although it has been more than four hundred years since the first Catholic missionary came to Japan, and more than one hundred years since the first Protestant missionaries brought the gospel into Japan, the percentage of Christians amongst the Japanese population is less than 1%.[1] It seems that Christianity has been either totally ignored, or rejected, by the Japanese.

Why do Japanese people not believe in the Gospel? It is an important task for ministers of the Gospel in Japan to examine the reasons for the stagnation of evangelism in this country, and to find effective strategies to win the Japanese for Christ.

The Pentecostal movement has, needless to say, been a powerful force in spreading the Gospel all over the world

---

[1] According to Christian Year Book 2004, the total number of Protestant churches is 8,083 and the number of members is 617,053. The Orthodox Church has 73 churches and 25,916 members. The Catholic Church has 1,027 churches and 477,624 members. The percentage of all Christians is 0.8%. The total population of Japan is about 127 million.

ever since its beginnings. Yet while this movement has impacted Christianity in Japan to some extent, it must be recognized that over 99% of Japanese have still not accepted Jesus Christ. Given that "[t]he priority or reason-for-being of the Assemblies of God is to be an agency for evangelizing the world," (Karkkainen, 2002) Japanese Pentecostalism should also be bearing the fruit of mission in Japan. The situation of Japan raises two important questions: Is there any advantage Pentecostals hold in Japanese evangelism? If so, what is the advantage of the Pentecostal mission?

In this book I will evaluate the Japanese world view and also consider the history of mission carried out by several Christian groups, to assist us in providing effective strategies to win more Japanese to Christ. We will consider the following questions:

1. What is the Japanese world view?

2. What was the mission approach of the Catholic and Protestant churches?

3. What was the mission approach of the Pentecostal churches?

4. What mission strategies could be effective for reaching Japanese?

I believe that this is a significant study in at least three ways. First, I personally can use the result of this research for my future ministry. I would like to have an underlying philosophy for my evangelism in Japan. Second, it may be of assistance for missionaries who are involved in the ministry in Japan to know the reality of mission in Japan and to have some hints to approach Japanese people. Third, this study might encourage Japanese Christians, especially the Pentecostal-Charismatic camp, to think about effective strategies for mission in Japan. I hope this book produces meaningful discussion regarding Christian mission in Japan.

The literature used in this book may be classified into three groups.

The first group deals with the Japanese mentality, both in general and in its religious philosophy. Benedict (1967) is a classic work, which deals with the Japanese mentality. She defines Japan as having a "culture of shame (*haji*)" and no concept of sin (*tsumi*) as found in the West. Doi (1971) is also a famous book, which provides a general analysis of the Japanese mentality. Doi uncovers the Japanese psychological phenomenon of *amae*, and asserts that one cannot understand the Japanese or Japanese culture without being aware of this concept. Ama (1999) and Yuasa (1999) both research in considerable depth the origin of Japanese religions and of Japanese religious thinking.

The second group of literature concerns the history of Japanese Christianity and the Japanese Pentecostal movement. Drummond (1971), Hiyane (1949) and Kaneda (1996) give meaningful and plentiful information about the history of Japanese Christianity. Regarding the history of Japanese Pentecostals, the Japan Assemblies of God (Japan AOG) has its own historical record, *Mikotoba ni Tachi, Mitama ni Michibikarete [Standing On the Word and Guided by the Spirit: The 50 Years History Since the Founding]* (1999). Although it deals with only the activities of the Japan Assemblies of God, it provides useful information about Japanese Pentecostal

3

history. Histories of pre-war Asian Pentecostal mission are only now beginning to be written. In fact, although many Pentecostal missionaries came and ministered to Japanese even before the war, they and their ministries were not widely known except by a few missionaries. However, this unknown history has recently been uncovered by scholars. Shew (2003) has just written *History of the Early Pentecostal Movement in Japan: The Roots and Development of the Pre-War Pentecostal Movement in Japan (1907-1945)* and his dissertation gives us much information concerning the early history of the Pentecostal Movement in Japan.

The third group consists of various theories of Christian mission in Japan. Furuya (2003) examines the reasons why the Japanese church is so stagnant. According to Furuya, most of those who first accepted the faith were taken from the former Samurai (warrior) classes. They were educated and influential but were not close to the middle and lower classes of Japanese, and this forms the biggest reason why Christianity did not become a common religion in Japan and why Christians are still in the minority. Finally, he suggests that we need to have a theology of Japan; in other words, a theology of Japanese evangelism, he believes, because Japan is the most difficult place in the world for evangelism. In Fukuda (2002), Sakurai (2002) asserts that Japanese Christianity is heavily influenced by Western methodology and theology. We must not regard Japanese culture as purely negative but find some elements in the culture through which Japanese can easily understand the gospel. Mandai (2000), as one of the influential young leaders of the Pentecostal camp in Japan, points out that we cannot use the strategies that work in the Western or majority worlds. In conclusion, he insists that we have to establish a new mission strategy, which is not seen in other countries. From the liberal camp, Kondo (2002, 2004) asserts the urgency of evangelism in Japan, and Goto (1959) deals with various theories of evangelism for Japan.

The suggested mission strategies that I will present target ordinary Japanese. The specific mission strategies I will discuss in this book must be modified by individual local churches, pastors, and members to suit their individual contexts. The historical research in this book will be limited to the history of Catholic mission in the 16th and 17th centuries and the history of Protestant mission after the 19th century. Although we have many Pentecostal organizations in Japan, I will write mainly concerning the Japan Assemblies of God.

We will begin our study with a survey of the Japanese worldview, which includes Japanese religious thinking and general mentalities, and we will consider literature related to the history of Japanese religions, and the sociology and psychology of the Japanese people. Chapters 3 and 4 will consist of a brief history of Japanese Christianity, and specifically the Pentecostal/Charismatic movement in Japan. We will try to uncover the strategies that there used to win Japanese to Christ, and then evaluate those strategies. Evaluating the above research, in chapter 5 we will develop effective mission strategies for Japan. The study will conclude with suggested methods for overcoming the challenges of mission in Japan.

Chapter 2

Japanese Worldview

In order to win people to Christ, we need to understand their worldview and religious thinking, and identify some of the characteristics of the way that people think. In this chapter, we will examine Japanese religious thinking, picking out some key concepts in the Japanese mentality which will help us to understand ordinary Japanese people. From these concepts we will list some challenges for Christian mission in Japan.

2.1 Religious Thinking

> The Japanese are among the most religious or least religious people on earth, depending on whom you talk to or how you define 'religious.' (Davis, 1992)

Much research and many observations about Japanese religious thinking prove this statement. While about 70%

of Japanese people think of themselves to be "non-religious" (*mu-shukyo*), (Ama, 1999:8, see also Ishii 1997:7) the total number of members of the various religions to which Japanese people belong actually adds up to a figure well over the total population of Japan![1]

For example, although in Japan, many Japanese (some 80% of the population) visit Shinto shrines for the blessing of the year (*hatsumode*) during New Year celebrations, (Kato, 1992:22) it is often said that when Japanese abroad are asked their religion, they are puzzled for an answer because many of them do not think of themselves as believing in any particular religion. (Ama 1999:11-12; Ishii 1997:124)

To understand Japanese religious thinking, we must know that there is a difference about the way that the concept of "religion" is used by ordinary Japanese and the way that it is used by Christians. If "being religious" means to believe in a particular doctrine like the Christian faith, then many Japanese do not think of themselves as religious. And yet, if it means to believe in something supernatural or something awesome, it would seem that many of them certainly are religious.

Hereinafter, I will present some characteristics of Japanese religious thinking.

2.1.1 Participation in religious events

First, ordinary Japanese respect participation in religious events more than they respect belief. For Japanese, participation in religious events, such as *hatsumode* (visiting a Shinto

---

[1] See Ishii 1997:17. According to this research, the total members of all the religious organizations are 215 million, while the total population of Japan is 126 million.

shrine during the first three days of January for a blessing for the year) and the *obon* Festival (a household memorial service for ancestors, held at the middle of August), is very important. In addition to these, there are many traditional rituals based on Japanese folk religion, such as special religious observances for pregnancy, birth (*omiya mairi*), early childhood (*shichi go san*), marriage, and death. (Soboku na Gimon Tankyukai [Simple Questions Research Association], 1998) It would seem that ordinary Japanese do not sense religious truth by knowing the teachings of religions, but rather sense religious truth by practicing religious ritual.

2.1.2   Plurality

Secondly, ordinary Japanese do not think it unnatural or not right to have plural religious affiliations.   Japanese people have long accepted other religions coming from other counties (mainly via the Korean Peninsula from China), adding them to their own folk religions. When they received a new faith tradition, Japanese did not deny their own folk religions but rather they changed the incoming faith to some extent so that they could easily incorporate it into their existing religious life.

For example, Japanese adopted Buddhism in the 6th century without denying Shinto—which was originally based on Japanese folk religion—and began to use the rituals of Buddhism for aspects of ancestor worship which Shinto could not adequately cover. (Ama 1999:50–55; Yuasa 1999:120; see also Osumi 1992) Although it seems that Christianity has been the only religion to strike against this Japanese religious pluralism—and hence has thus been rejected—some events from Christianity such as Christmas and St. Valentine's Day

9

are now deeply rooted into Japanese life. Ordinary Japanese do not think it a contradiction to go to shrines over New Year, just one week after they have celebrated Christmas.

2.1.3 Sense of belonging

Thirdly, Japanese gain a sense of belonging by participating in religious rituals. In other words, for the Japanese, religions (Shinto and Buddhism) have been the ties that formed the village community and the household. Japanese have been obliged to belong to two groups: firstly to the local village community (*mura*), and secondly to a household (*ie*). Shinto shrines have been the center of each village community. Buddhist temples have been the facilitator of ancestor worship. As previously mentioned, however, the main reasons for participation in these rituals are not based upon beliefs inherent in the religions, but out of a kind of social pressure. Mark R. Mullins, a professor at Meiji Gakuin University, analyzes the situation as follows:

> Most Japanese naturally participated in the annual festivals and rituals of the local Shinto shrine and Buddhist temple. Participation in religious events and rituals was primarily motivated by the sense of duty and obligation that accompanied membership in a household and community, not by clearly defined beliefs or exclusive creeds. (Mullins, 1998:7–8)

We can therefore say that Japanese religious thinking is closely related to the sense of social belonging.

2.1.4   Worldly benefits (goriyaku)

Fourthly, Japanese religious thinking tends to seek after worldly benefits (*goriyaku*). (Katsumoto, 1990:38) Japanese, for instance, get talismans (a small bag thought to have magical powers to bring good luck) from temples and shrines to help them with their school entrance examinations, for road safety, having an easy birth, healing, prosperity in business, and for other life events.

While Japan has become one of the most developed countries in the world, many folk beliefs and superstitions still affect Japanese thinking and acting. For instance, the ages 25 and 42 for men and 19 and 33 for women are thought to be the years that an individual is most likely to experience calamities or misfortunes (*yakudoshi*). (Eibun Nihon Daijiten [English-Japanese Dictionary], 1996:226-7) To avoid such misfortunes, many people of those ages go to the shrines to be prayed for or to get talismans. Divination is popular among many Japanese. Words or expressions associated with or considered to bring bad luck are strongly avoided. It is not unusual to see Japanese people do something purely for luck.

2.2   Japanese Social Mentality

2.2.1   Group Orientation

> The Japanese, in short, are almost the perfect "organization men." (Reischauer, 1972:132)

Without understanding the sense of belonging to a group, it is difficult to understand the mentality of typical Japanese.

The system of Japanese society essentially forces Japanese people to belong to some community. As mentioned before, religion has played a significant role in making people belong to a local community (*mura*) and family (*ie*). It can also be said that Japan's agricultural heritage has made the Japanese group-oriented. This sense of belonging has been deeply rooted into Japanese minds. For Japanese, the idea of being isolated from their groups is a very fearful thought.

Although industrialization and urbanization may seem to have released the Japanese, particularly those living in the big cities, from this sense of being bound to a village community and even to a family, most Japanese still find themselves being bound to other groups: school and neighborhood cliques, clubs in and out of school, and groups in the workplace. The concept of group identity persists as the basis of the Japanese social structure. Belonging to a group is a normal phenomenon for human beings and can be seen in every place of the world. For Japanese, however, the sense of group belonging is considerably more pronounced and more important than it would be to Westerners.

Japanese people seek to find their value by playing a significant part in the group to which they belong. This is sometimes described as *ikigai*, one's sense of power over one's life. "Japanese firstly get a feeling of relief from having an intimate relationship, one in which they can make demands of each other without fearing rejection, and also find their *ikigai* (worth) by maintaining such relationships." (Hamaguchi, 1982:88) For this reason, Japanese hold others' valuation of themselves in high esteem. It is often said that Japanese are "workaholics." While it may be that they truly like to work, many of them are always thinking of others in their workplaces.

12

They have to work hard because they do not want to become a nuisance to others or because they want to be valued by others. "Each Japanese seems to be constantly worrying about what the other person thinks of him." (Reischauer, 1972:143)

Because of this group oriented nature, Japanese respect harmony in the group and tend to avoid conflict with others. They will sometimes conceal their feelings in order to maintain the harmony of the group, because causing friction within a group is regarded as evil conduct.

2.2.2 Shame

Since Japanese do not have the concept of an absolute God and see themselves primarily as members of groups, their ethical standards are different from those of Christians. In a sense, Japanese ethics are more relativistic or situational than universal. (Reischauer, 1972:139) Japanese tend to base their principles of conduct on other people because they "worry that they may not be doing the right thing and thus are opening themselves to criticism or ridicule by others." (p. 143) The root of this thought is a sense of shame.

In classifying cultures into "guilt cultures" and "shame cultures," Ruth Benedict, an anthropologist, asserts that Japanese culture is a typical shame culture. Although there are some who do not agree with her definition, (Hamaguchi, 1982:61–62) her assertions are broadly admitted. The sense of shame more or less controls the entirety of Japanese conduct. This attitude may be nurtured even from childhood. Most parents discipline their children by indicating that their behavior is shameful rather than sinful.

It is not fair to say that Japanese do not have a sense of guilt, but it is clear that their sense of guilt is not based on God, but on the judgement of others. Takeo Doi, a psychiatrist, points out that "it is characteristic that the Japanese sense of guilt is sharply revealed when they feel that they disappoint their group." (Doi, 1971:63) While Westerners feel guilt in terms of their relationship with God, Japanese sense it within their relationships with others in their group.

When a child becomes a Christian in Japan, it is not uncommon for his or her parents to oppose their decision. One of the biggest reasons for this is that Christians do not attend ancestor worship rituals. We cannot, however, consider that all such parents are fervent believers in the teaching of Buddhism; rather, it seems that many of them think that if their child does not attend the ceremony, they may be shamed by other relatives.

2.2.3 Nonverbal Communication

Japanese society is highly homogenous. They speak and read the same language and always live in an environment made up of group membership. Therefore, nonverbal communication such as etiquette and gestures has developed in sophistication as a significant portion of the communication between individuals. (Eibun Nihon Daijiten [English-Japanese Dictionary], 1996:84–85) The bow (*ojigi*), for example, plays an essential role as a medium communication: even its depth or speed can express a feeling and represent the relationship between two people.

The development of nonverbal communication, in other words, means that the Japanese are not good at using verbal communication. Many of them do not have the skill of debate and speech as found in the West, and rather tend to avoid using strong verbal interaction as a means to persuade others. When there is a difference of opinion between two people, some exercise silence to reflect their objection rather than insist on their thought. Usually, the goal of decision making is not a majority decision, but reaching a consensus in which everyone comes to a general agreement and no one continues to hold strong objections. (Reischauer, 1972:135)

One of the problems of evangelism to such people is that they are not used to being persuaded with clear verbal interaction. Needless to say, when non-Japanese and often even Japanese Christians evangelize the Japanese people, their communication is normally verbal. Japanese, however, respect nonverbal communication. We have to consider whether or not our communication skills with Japanese are happening in an essentially Western manner. Even if we teach them the concepts of Creator God, sin, salvation, eternity, and so on, they may not be able to accept those ideas with much depth because they are not moved by verbal interaction. We may need something beyond verbal interaction.

2.2.4   Human Relationships

Finally, let us look at some basic concepts of human relationships in Japan.

Chie Nakane, an anthropologist, defined Japanese society as a vertical society. According to her, human relations can be divided into two categories, "vertical" and "horizontal," and for Japanese, the vertical human relation is the structural principle in uniting the members of a group.   (Nakane,

15

1972:30) "Age, power, sex, rank, role, and experience are the outstanding qualities differentiating superiors and subordinates in most societies." (Eibun Nihon Daijiten [English-Japanese Dictionary], 1996:76–77) Japanese society contains many vertical diadic relationships, such as that of teacher (*sensei*) and student (*seito*), senior (*sempai*) and junior (*kohai*), parent (*oya*) and child (*ko*), supervisor (*joshi*) and subordinate (*buka*), and so on. They are unconsciously aware of these positions, and there is an unwritten rule that the subordinates cannot oppose the superiors. This, at the same time, does not necessarily lead to repressive or reluctant human relationships. The superiors often offer their assistance and advice to the subordinates, and the subordinates respect and follow the superiors and sometimes offer their personal loyalty. This type of framework of human relationships can be found at all levels and in all areas of Japanese life.

The consciousness that the subordinates have with respect to their superiors is often described as *on*. "*On* actually means the benevolence or favor of the ruler, feudal lord, or parent but has been turned around in most usage to signify the unlimited debt of gratitude or obligation of the recipient to the bestower of this grace." (Reischauer, 1972:141) Today, the bestower is not only a person but also a group such as a company. This concept of *on* is important for Japanese. It is broadly and deeply held that a person who receives *on* from somebody has to repay this obligation. If a person requites *on* with ingratitude, he or she has to be accused and will be publicly shamed.

On the other hand, there is also the concept of *amae*. Takeo Doi asserts that *amae* is the key concept for understanding the social structure of Japan. (Doi, 1971:40) *Amae*, which can be translated as "a desire for dependency," is the noun form of *amaeru*, a verb that has no true equivalent in English but refers to the desire to depend upon the love, patience, and tolerance of others. (Eibun Nihon Daijiten [English-Japanese Dictionary], 1996:92–93)

In a group, Japanese have strong feelings of intimacy and sometimes loyalty to the group and its members. They feel close to their group and try to repay obligations within it. At the same time, they have the desire to be accepted and loved by the group and the other members. They believe that both the group and its individual members should love and accept them even if they make a mistake or lack something. This feeling is *amae*. Japanese use feelings of both *on* and *amae* to maintain their relationships with others.

At any rate, it is clear that the Japanese mentality is deeply rooted within a group orientation. When Japanese people feel shame, their shame concerns their standing with their group. In a group, nonverbal communication can work particularly well, and they can maintain human relationships based on vertical relations. Both *on* and *amae* should be recognized within the group context.

2.3 Summary and Challenges for Christian Mission

There seems to be no concept of the Absolute in Japanese religious thinking. Traditionally, Japanese have accepted any religious tradition into their culture (except for Christianity) and even modified their teachings. For most Japanese, a religious truth is not one that they have to follow, but something that they can employ for their own benefit. It is difficult for Japanese with their mindset to grant that there is one Absolute and only God who rules everything. This point must be the biggest challenge for Christian mission.

The Japanese way of recognizing religious truth is also totally different from that of Westerners. Japanese accept or understand religious truth not by intellectual studying but by participating in rituals. Unless they participate and experience something, they never believe in the truth. Experience is very important for them. We have to think about the way to approach Japanese. Do we try to make Japanese understand truth by intellectual teaching or by experiencing truth? Do the Pentecostals have some advantage on this point?

Another significant point of Japanese religious thinking is that for Japanese the importance of believing in a religion is connected to the importance of belonging to a community. Belonging to a household means believing in Buddhism. Belonging to a village community means believing in Shinto. Ordinary Japanese cannot separate a religion from a community or group they belong to, and vice versa. This fact causes us to think how we try to attract people. It can be easily imagined that, without presenting a community to which they can belong, it might be difficult for Japanese to join a Christian circle.

Our research into the Japanese mentality also shows that Japanese are a strongly group oriented people. Their worldview is firmly derived from their group oriented nature. Since they do not have the concept of an Absolute, they need to calibrate their values based on the viewpoints of others. They do not recognize the concept of sin that the Bible teaches. Instead, they believe that they have to avoid whatever

18

would cause them to be criticized by others because it would be shameful for them. Their ethical standard is sometimes situational, rather than universal.

I would like to conclude as follows: there may be two main difficulties in planting the seed of the Christian Gospel into the Japanese mind. One is that Japanese have no concept of the Absolute. The other is that Japanese religions are closely related to the community.

It is a considerable challenge that the Japanese have no concept of the Absolute. The truth of the Bible cannot be understood without understanding that God is the Absolute who has created everything and who dominates everything, even the history of human beings. How can we help Japanese recognize the absolute God?

The fact that Japanese are very group oriented people seems to be one of the big challenges to win them. For the ordinary Japanese, to become a Christian may well mean leaving their communities, such as their household or village community. However, some keys concepts in the Japanese mentality, such as nonverbal communication, the sense of shame, vertical relations, and the concepts of *on* and *amae*, can be useful tools for mission. The point is to connect this Japanese mentality with an understanding of the Gospel.

In chapters three and four, I will examine what past Christian churches have done in Japan. How did they make efforts to overcome these challenges, and to what degree were they effective?

Chapter 3

History of Japanese Christianity

In this chapter, I will briefly outline the history of Japanese Christianity, (Catholic groups in the 16th and 17th centuries and Protestant churches from the 19th Century). and then examine their mission strategies. How did they try to win the Japanese for the Lord? How did the Japanese regard Christianity? How did the Japanese accept the Gospel?

3.1 A Brief History of Roman Catholicism (16th-17th Centuries)

The mid-sixteenth century, when European missionaries came to Japan, was one of the most turbulent periods in Japan's history. (Fujita, 1991:3)

In this period, every authority and system which had been maintaining order in society collapsed—the Emperor, the nobles and the Shogun. There were many independent kingdoms within Japan at that time, and the *daimyo*s (feudal lords) were fighting against each other to unify the whole country. This 'Warring State' Period continued until the beginning of the 17th century when the Tokugawa Shogunate was established.

The life of the people was hard. The main employment was agriculture but the long civil war destroyed many fields and houses. Some people had to abandon their land and become refugees. Once, there was such a severe famine that it led people to abandon or even kill their children so that they could survive. (Ebisawa and Saburo, 1970:18)

Under such situations, a pessimistic view of the world broadly spread among the people. At the same time, however, corruption of religious power became obvious. Buddhism lost its power for directing the religious life of the people, and many priests became worldly and sought after their own pleasure. (p. 21) Some Buddhism temples became armouries as certain Buddhist groups (particularly *Jodo Shinshu*) banded together and openly rebelled against their lords, an uprising called the *Ikko Ikki*. In general, the contemporary religions could not comfort those who were suffering the harsh realities of life. The message of Christianity came to Japan at that time.

The first person who brought the message of Christianity into Japan was Francis Xavier (1506-1552), a Jesuit. Before Xavier arrived in Japan, he met a Japanese man named Yajiro at Malacca. Xavier realized the man's intelligence and thought Japanese people were intelligent enough to possibly respond to Christian preaching. He considered the possibility of opening a mission in Japan. (Shiono, 1997:13) In 1549, he arrived at Kagoshima, in southern Japan, and from there Xavier launched his ministry. He went to Kyoto, where the Emperor and the aristocracy were, and attempted to evangelize them. However, they had substantially lost their authority and Xavier did not accomplish his aim.

After that, Xavier focused his efforts on Yamaguchi, in the west of Japan. In spite of much oppression, his ministry successfully gained some five hundred converts in about two months. (Fujita, 1991:32) Later Xavier and his co-workers went to Bungo, a part of Kyushu, and continued to minister there. He laid the foundation of the church and left Japan in 1551.

Xavier's successors, Torres and Fernandez, also succeeded in winning many Japanese and establishing schools, hospitals, orphanages and other such institutions. Later, the Franciscans also came to Japan and started their own ministry in the 1590s. It is reported that there were 350,000 believers in 1580 and 600,000 in 1600. (Nakamura, 1965) Some of the *daimyo* became Christians and encouraged their people to accept their belief.

The primary reason why Christianity grew so fast is that the new leaders of Japan, Nobunaga Oda (1534-1582) and Hideyoshi Toyotomi (1536-1598)—who were trying to unify Japan and almost succeeded in their efforts—protected the missionaries' activities. However, we must not ignore the fact that these leaders had ambitions to utilize missionaries for trade, especially guns, with European countries. After Hideyoshi Toyotomi attained his conquest of the whole of Japan, he regarded Christianity as useless and even an obstacle to his rule.

In 1587, Hideyoshi announced the deportation of missionaries from Japan. Christian *daimyo*s were commanded to abandon their faith. If they did not obey this command, their territories would be confiscated. This was the beginning of the persecution of Christianity. And yet this prohibition was relatively loosely applied because Hideyoshi was still attracted to making a profit through trade with the Westerners. The missionaries could still continue their work, but in secret.

Ieyasu Tokugawa (1542-1616), who grasped power in the country after the death of Hideyoshi, took over Hideyoshi's policy of oppressing Christianity and strengthened it. He regarded Christianity as dangerous to his rule and considered it necessary to close the country in order to maintain his dynasty. In 1614, he proclaimed the total prohibition of the Christian faith. All the missionaries were compelled to go out to Macao or Manila together with several famous Christian *daimyo*s and their families. Tokugawa closed the country (*sakoku*) to cement his rule and shut the door to Christianity. The government hunted down Christians and forced them to abandon their faith. If they refused to renounce their beliefs, they were tortured and killed. Under this violent storm, Christianity was dealt a deadly blow. This anti-Christian policy firmly rooted in the Japanese mind the idea that the Christian faith is dangerous and repugnant. (Drummond, 1971:124–125) Tokugawa also used Buddhism to further exclude Christianity. All the Japanese were required to register their birth, marriages, and deaths at a local Buddhist temple (the *tera-uke* system, see, e.g., Mullins 1998:7).

It seemed that the light of the Christian faith had been snuffed out. However, it is astonishing to think that some Christians remained hidden and passed on their faith to

24

their offspring until Japan opened its borders in 1858. After Japan was once again opened up, Christian missionaries began to come and rebuild the church, even though officially the government maintained the prohibition of Christianity. In 1865, several Japanese visited a Christian missionary and one of them, an old woman said, "The hearts of all of us here are the same as yours." They were the descendants of Christians. (Ebisawa and Saburo 1970:158; Fujita 1991:244)

3.2   Mission Strategies of the Catholic Groups

From the history outlined above, we can say that mission in Japan in the 16th century by Catholic groups was a great success, in spite of the short period in which it was undertaken. How did they win over the Japanese?

3.2.1   Targeting the Lords

Wherever Xavier went, he first met the lords (*daimyo*) there and asked for permission to form a mission. At the same time, he preached the Gospel to the *daimyo*. His successors also did so, because they thought if the lords there became the believers, they would be effective in evangelizing the native people. (Goto 1959:50; Suzuki 2001b:23) Practically they succeeded in converting quite a few *daimyo*. As mentioned previously, some of the Christian *daimyo* were purely interested in trade with Portugal and in the technologies of the Westerners. There were several who gave up their faith when Hideyoshi prohibited the Christian faith. Some of them, however, never abandoned their faith, even when they were forced to surrender their territories and leave the country.[1]

At any rate, Christian mission in the areas where the local lord was a believer was particularly successful. It was often observed that whole villages converted to the Christian faith.

3.2.2   Social Works

In the time of the long civil war, the possessions of the people had been plundered and there was no concept of social welfare. It is natural that the social works of the Catholic groups proved attractive to many Japanese. Some groups, for instance, actively built asylums for the aged, as well as orphanages, refugee camps, and hospitals. They also worked as gravediggers, a job which people were reluctant to do themselves, and they redeemed slaves and prostitutes from their lifestyles. (Ebisawa and Saburo, 1970:53) The people were amazed and pleased with the missionaries' social works.

The Christian faith influenced Japanese ethics as well. In those days, homosexuality was broadly accepted in the society of samurai and even among the Buddhist priests. In addition, it was noted that the lords kept many mistresses. The missionaries strongly denounced them and asserted the value of monogamy. Christian ethics were effective in evangelizing the intelligentsia. In particular, many wives of daimyo and the high class samurai were moved by the teachings of Christianity and came to believe in them. The ideas of respecting marriage, child care, and home life had never been seen in Japan before. (*ibid*, p. 73)

[1]Famous Christian daimyo, Ukon Takayama and Juan Naito, were forced to go to the Philippines where they died at Manila. See, e.g. Drummond 1971:96.

3.2.3 Education

The missionaries contributed to the education of the native people. In those days, almost all of the people were illiterate. The missionaries built schools for children and first taught them the alphabet. There were about 200 Catholic schools in 1580, all in the Western part of Japan. (*ibid*, p. 55) In the schools, the children studied not only Catholic doctrine but also Portuguese, mathematics, music, painting, and other subjects.

The missionaries also established seminaries and colleges to train national Christian leaders. The level of learning seems to have been quite high. The college provided a basis course and a major course. The basis course included liberal arts and music, art and drama. The major course had theology and philosophy and the study of Japanese religion, literature, language and culture. (*ibid*, p. 56)

They published many books about Christian doctrine and the Christian life. For example, the *Japanese Catechism of The Christian Faith* consists of two volumes covering the following topics:

> Volume 1: (1) polemical discussion on the Japanese religions, (2) Deus, (3) cosmology, (4) Buddhism, (5) Buddhist ethics, (6) the principal doctrines of Christianity, (7) the Trinity.
>
> Volume 2: (1) the Decalogue, (2) the sacrament, (3) the resurrection of the dead and the last judgment, (4) Heaven and Hell. (Fujita, 1991:83)

These publications were effective tools for educating and strengthening the believers.

3.2.4 Grouping

The believers formed groups (*kumi*) to take care and help each other. This group activity played a significant role in spreading the faith and maintaining it. (Ebisawa and Saburo, 1970:71) They had strict rules within the group and chose leaders from among themselves. The leader read the catechism in the group meeting and taught the members. They also did social work for the weak.

After the persecution began, the class of *daimyo* and samurai could not maintain their faith but some lower class members among the believers were able to keep their faith in secret. As previously mentioned, the faith of most believers seemed to perish under the severe policy instigated during the Tokugawa Shogunate, but astonishingly some of them retained their faith and passed it on to their children. They pretended to be Buddhists while maintaining their faith underground for a long time.

Needless to say, the biggest reason why some Japanese Christians managed to uphold their faith is that they had a support structure in the *kumi* group and hence could encourage one another through the persecution.

3.3 Catholic Mission Strategies: Its Strengths and Weaknesses

The Catholic missionaries, Xavier and his successors, studied Japanese culture, tradition, worldview, life style, and religions in depth as they tried to reach out to the Japanese. They did not deny nor reject the Japanese culture, but rather they respected it. Such an attitude seemed to gain a good reputation among the native people. "This method intended to cautiously evaluate the local tradition, culture, and social conditions and skillfully adapt Christian evangelism to these given factors." (Fujita, 1991:145)

The Catholic missionaries tried to meet the needs of the Japanese. In those days, knowledge belonged only to such people as samurai and Buddhism priests. Ordinary people only had the opportunity of education and welfare provision due to the mission of the Catholics. Furthermore the upper class also had the benefit of trade with Portugal. Through this they were exposed to Western culture and were attracted to it.

The system of grouping, as mentioned before, was an effective ministry for mission in Japan. In particular, it played a significant role during the era of persecution. We can say that this mission strategy met the needs of the group-oriented nature of Japanese.

On the other hand, the position of the missionaries was too close to Japan's political leaders. At the beginning, this close relationship with the leaders was positive and it led to successful results for the mission. Later, however, the relationship worsened and caused significant problems for the mission. When the leader of Japan brought in a new anti-Christian policy, for example, the missionaries' approach had to change dramatically. The political leaders Hideyoshi and Ieyasu believed that Western ambition toward Japan lay behind Christianity. As mentioned before, after these leaders conquered the whole country, Christianity became useless and indeed rather dangerous to them.

There also seemed to be conflict among the missionaries. After Hideyoshi proclaimed the prohibition of Christian mission in 1587, the Franciscans arrived in 1592. There was antagonism between the Jesuits from Portugal and the Franciscans from Spain. While the Jesuits claimed a monopoly on Japanese mission (Fujita, 1991:127) and tried to not to attract Hideyoshi's attention, the Franciscans started their own mission openly. What is more, there were other conflicts between the Catholic group and the Protestant traders from Holland and England, some of which happened in front of the political Japanese leaders. (*ibid*, p. 146) This disunited attitude among Christians caused a sense of caution among the political leaders of Japan.

3.4 A History of Protestant Groups in the 19th and 20th Centuries

After a long period of national isolation, Japan finally opened its door to the West in 1858. This decision was not necessarily voluntary; rather it was a reluctant determination that took place against the background of forceful Western oppression. In fact, this change of policy weakened the Tokugawa Shogunate; the other powers raised an army against the Shogunate and eventually overturned the Tokugawa dynasty.

The biggest and the most urgent challenge for the new government was to establish a modern country so that they could avoid being colonized by the West. During this time—known as the Meiji Restoration—the role of the emperor, who had been powerless under the Tokugawa Shogunate, was made central to the new unified country, and the aim was to create a Shinto-centered system of government. (Reischauer, 1972:218)

Most of all, the Japanese were at the mercy of rapid social change. In particular, all of the samurai lost their jobs and their privileges. In the midst of such chaos, people had to find a new life.

3.4.1   Mainline Protestants

Alhough Christianity was still strictly prohibited, in 1859 the first Protestant missionaries, John Liggins (1829-1912) and Channing M. Williams (1829-1910) came to Japan; they belonged to the U.S. Anglican church. (Saito, 1981:111) After them, many missionaries belonging to the Presbyterian, Dutch Reformed, and other churches arrived in Japan. They mainly studied Japanese and taught English, and they engaged in medical treatment and setting up mission schools. In 1865, the first Japanese Protestant believer was baptized in secret. (*ibid*, p. 45)

In 1873, the Japanese government finally permitted missionaries to evangelize openly. In the 1880s, Japanese churches forcefully advanced. There was an internal reason and an external reason for this. The internal reason was that Japanese ministers who had studied at missionaries' Bible schools graduated and began to build churches and publish a Japanese Bible and hymn books. The external reason was due to the policy of the government. They positively tried to introduce Western culture into Japan to catch up with Western countries. This situation drew the Japanese people into churches. In 1885, there were 168 churches and 11,000 Christians. After five years, in 1890, there were 300 churches and 34,000 Christians. (*ibid*)

However, in the 1890s, Japanese churches met with a variety of difficulties.

First, the Japanese government changed their policy. Shintoism became the state religion. They began to build a national polity based on the concept that the Japanese Emperor is god (*kami*) and that all Japanese people would gather in allegiance to the Emperor. Naturally, this policy was not compatible with the Christian faith. Second, until that time, the theology of the missionaries had been basically conservative, and they respected the authority of the Bible. However, in the 1890s, German and American missionaries introduced modernist thinking to Japanese churches. (*ibid*) It was called "new theology (*shin-shingaku*);" in other words, liberal theology. Japanese church leaders were theologically immature at the time, and so liberal theology shook leaders' faith. Many of them left their faith due to the influence of the new theology.

3.4.2 Evangelicals (Holiness Movement)

As the source of the Japanese evangelical camp, we need to consider the mission of the Japan Evangelistic Band led by Barclay Buxton and the Holiness Movement led by Juji Nakada.

Barclay Fowell Buxton (1860-1946), who eventually introduced the British Perfectionist movement and the Keswick "Higher Life" movement to the Japanese Church, came to Japan in 1890.

Buxton went neither to Tokyo nor to Osaka, but to Matsue, a remote city in the western part of Japan where he established his ministry. He established a Bible school there. Many promising Japanese young men came to Matsue and studied. Buxton's ministry was called the "Matsue Band," and became the source of the Holiness movement in Japan. (Kudo, 1965)

In 1903, Buxton established the Japan Evangelistic Band with his co-worker Paget Wilkes. In 1905, they moved to Kobe. They had a broad range of ministries, which included building a Bible School, building a base for evangelism, and holding conventions for ministers and missionaries.

Juji Nakada (1870-1939), the founder of Japan Holiness Church, studied at Moody Bible Institute and came back to Japan in 1898. At first, Nakada was appointed a traveling evangelist in the Methodist Church, though his preaching extended beyond Methodist churches. In 1901, after meeting Charles and Lettie Cowman who were the first ordained missionaries in the Pilgrim Holiness Church, Nakada resigned from the Methodist Church. Nakada and the Cowmans built the Central Evangelical House at Tokyo which would emphasize the holiness teaching.

In 1905, Nakada and the Cowmans formed the Oriental Missionary Society together with Ernest Kilbourne and Tetsusaburo Sasao. Later, this society became the OMS Holiness Church in Japan in 1917. (Holiness Conference North America, 2003)

The Japan Holiness Church experienced two revivals, in 1919 and 1930. The following table shows the results of those revivals. (Holiness Band Showa Kirisutokyo Danatsushi Kankokai, 1983:7)

The Japanese Church that had been stagnating due to liberal theology was dramatically affected by these two

Table 3.1: Revivals in the Japan Holiness Church

Year	Churches	Members (Pastors)	Being baptized
1928	160	8,400 (213)	1950
1930	330	12,000 (310)	4311
1932	434	19,523 (400)	2882

"bands", the Japan Evangelistic Band led by Buxton and the Holiness Church led by Juji Nakada. These bands respected the authority of the Bible and emphasized the power of the Holy Spirit. They also earnestly sought for revival in Japan. These elements created good soil for the arrival of the Pentecostal message.

3.4.3 The War

Japan succeeded in its programme of modernisation, and over the course of several wars, Japan finally became one of the great world powers. However, an incident with China, which occurred in 1931, left the country's international relationships in deadlock and Japan's relationship with the U.S. and England progressively worsened. Warfare with the West seemed to be inevitable. The wartime government needed to control every aspect of national life, even within the realm of religion, in order to compel the people to go to battle. The government forced all of the Protestant churches to form and join one denomination so that they could be controlled easily. In June 1941, under strict instructions from the government, The United Church of Christ in Japan was established. It included 34 Protestant denominations, and its total membership was more than 250,000. (Nakamura, 2003:143)

During the war, the life of Christians came under serious hardship. All the people were compelled to worship at the state Shinto shrine to pray for the victory of the nation. The Christians who refused underwent considerable social pressure. Some of pastors fell under suspicion of political rebellion and were arrested by the police. In particular, the Holiness churches went through severe persecutions. Over a hundred pastors were arrested and at least seven died in prison. (Holiness Band Showa Kirisutokyo Danatsushi Kankokai, 1983:iv) The churches that continued to meet were very few.

In August 1945, Japan was defeated and the Pacific War was over. The Christian Church finally received the freedom to evangelise, and many missionaries came back to Japan. The occupying army took a favourable attitude toward the Church, and assistance such as foods and clothes were sent to the Church in Japan from Canada and the U.S. (Ebisawa and Saburo, 1970:606)

In the first few years after the War, Japanese Christian churches experienced good growth. People came to the church to experience American culture and to receive supplies. Yet it still seemed that the Church could not help the Gospel to take root in Japanese society. After Japan gained independence again in 1951, the growth of Christianity halted. (Suzuki, 2001b:194) On the whole, while the number of churches and members have been increasing slightly over the years since the War, the reality is that Christians still make up less than 1% of the Japanese population.

3.5 Mission Strategies of Protestant Groups

3.5.1 A New Thought: Discipline and Ethics

Christianity brought new concepts to Japan, such as freedom, equality, and philanthropy. (*ibid*, p. 101) These kinds of thoughts were very new to the Japanese who had been living under a feudal society. The Christian church also produced the concept of disciplinary ethics, such as honesty, sincerity, diligence, integrity, and stoicism. (*ibid*)

As previously mentioned, the social class most influenced by the Meiji Restoration was the samurai. They lost all of the privileges that they had had, and the Restoration literally changed their understanding of life. "When Protestant Christianity came in through American missionaries in the 19th Century, the people who received the message were mainly the children of the former samurai." (Furuya, 2003:62) For them, Christianity provided a philosophy and ethics by which to live. Originally, samurai had been educated by a strict code of self-discipline, (*bushido*) but the social upheaval of the Meiji Restoration left them confused and disappointed. They found that Christianity could provide alternative disciplinary ethics. One of the more influential leaders of the church, Kanzo Uchimura, emphasized a "Christianity that grafted in *Bushido*," and other leaders also tried to join the Christian faith together with the philosophy of *bushido*. (*ibid*, pp. 62–79)

Since the former Samurai were generally more educated and formed the dominant class in the society, their activities as Christians were influential.

3.5.2   English and Education

The development of a new civilization caused the people to turn to English and education. The Church played a significant role in both English teaching and education. Needless to say, both ministries were effective mission strategies to win the hearts of the Japanese. Missionaries opened English schools and many who wanted to study English came. (Suzuki, 2001b:84) Mission boards established many Christian schools.

The influence that Christianity has made on the modern Japanese educational system is inestimable. In particular, Christianity opened the door to girls' education. Under the feudal society, most women were not allowed to study. The Church founded many girls' schools after the missionaries arrived. (see *ibid*, pp. 86–87) Indeed, "most of the women's high schools before the War and more than ten percent of all the Universities after the War were Christian schools."(Furuya, 2003:31)

3.5.3   Social Work and Welfare

We cannot deny that Japanese Christianity took an active part in social work and welfare. For instance, Ashio Kodaku, the first person who dealt with the problem of pollution, was a Christian. Many Christians participated in the first labor movement in Japan. (Suzuki, 2001b:136–137) The anti-prostitution movement was also led by many Christians. (*ibid*, p. 144)

Thus, Christianity contributed to the modernization of Japan and the enlightenment of the Japanese people.

3.6 Protestant Mission Strategies: Its Strengths and Weaknesses

3.6.1 Strengths

It can be argued that the early Protestant missionaries tried to meet the needs of the Japanese. They provided what was needed for the modernization of the country. They gave new thought to moral ethical standard and education, based on Christianity. The Church provided what the Japanese did not have during the feudal era, such as freedom, equality, and philanthropy. The ideas of Christianity also strongly influenced the new Japanese leaders in their promotion of modern social structures. The Church also contributed to the recovery of Japan after the war which had completely destroyed Japan. "The whole history of modern Japan... is inextricably linked with the presence of the Christian witness and fellowship in its midst." (Drummond, 1971:363)

Although during the militaristic era Christians were persecuted as spies of the enemies or as radical elements against the government, it seems that the whole society of Japan came to accept the presence of Christianity. At least, we do not see an antagonistic attitude against Christianity any more in Japanese society. This is a credit to the efforts of missionaries and senior Christians, as during the rule of the Tokugawa Shogunate, the idea that Christianity was a dangerous religion had been deeply planted into the minds of the Japanese for more than 200 years. The negative impression towards Christianity seems to have been totally removed from Japanese minds. This reality is clearly a positive development for future mission in Japan.

3.6.2 Weaknesses

Although Japanese have complete freedom to evangelize and have made much positive influence upon society, the total population believers make up less than one percent of the entire Japanese population. Why do Japanese people not come into the Church? I would like to present three main reasons for this: the church's knowledge-centeredness, its clergy (minister)-centeredness, and its lack of contextualization.

It seems that Japanese Christianity gives the impression to the people that Christianity is a knowledge-centered religion. As previously mentioned, Japanese Christianity first spread among the former samurai class; they were the intelligentsia and the leaders of society. Although this is the primary reason why Christianity has had an impact on the whole of Japanese society, at the same time, Christianity has not become a religion of the grass roots. As noted in chapter two, for ordinary Japanese, religious experience is important. However, "it seems that the scholastic approach determined the character of the Church in Japan and still prevails today." (Nagasawa, 2002)

Related to the above, the Japanese church, which has spread among the former *samurai*, has been a clergy-centered church. (Furuya, 2003:107–108) Japanese call a pastor *sensei*, which is mainly used to refer to a school teacher. As seen in chapter two, there are some strong vertical relationships in the Japanese consciousness. The relationship between teacher and student is one of them. While there may be a positive side to this, a negative element is that ordinary believers do not feel they can do anything without their pastor's permission or guidance. In other words, a pastor has to do everything and members normally just listen to the pastor's preaching. This tradition seems to form the basic expectation that only the pastors evangelize and the members simply attend services.

I would also like to highlight the lack of contextualization in Japanese Christianity as one of the weaknesses of the Protestant mission strategies. In fact, there seems to be a tendency that Japanese Christians (especially the Evangelical camp and Pentecostal/Charismatic camp) regard Japanese culture as simple idolatry and Western culture as 'Christian'. This seems to be the influence of missionaries' teaching. Mitsuo Fukuda, president of Rethinking Authentic Christianity Network, wonders

> how many opportunities for missionary evangelism must have been lost because the missionary rejected the Japanese culture, considering it pagan, thinking that the Japanese culture had to be radically rectified (or that another culture had to replace it!) (Fukuda, 2001:142)

Many such troubles were caused by a lack of comprehension of the Japanese culture by the Western missionaries in Japanese mission. For instance, "converts were often encouraged to burn their family altars and ancestral tablets to witness to their acceptance of Christ." (Smith 1974, cited in Boyle 1986) If such a thing happens, the family will never open their hearts to the gospel.

Chapter 4

History of Japanese Pentecostalism

In this chapter, I will mainly focus on the pre-history and history of the Japan Assemblies of God (AoG), because the Japan AoG is one of the groups which has the longest history in the Japanese Pentecostal movement and is the biggest Pentecostal denomination in Japan, although there were many people who were not included in the official AoG history.

4.1   General History of Japanese Pentecostalism

The Pentecostal faith directly came to Japan from the Azusa Street Revival in America. The first missionaries who brought the Pentecostal message to Japan were Martin L. Ryan and his group. Ryan went to Azusa Street in 1906 and experienced baptism in the Holy Spirit. He began to minister in Spokane, Washington. The congregation soon experienced baptism in the Holy Spirit and felt led to go into mission in East Asia. (Shew, 2002:29) Ryan and his group arrived in Japan in late September 1907. (*ibid*, p. 30) They ministered primarily in Tokyo and Yokohama but their stay was somewhat short. Some of the team members went back to the U.S., and some went on to China (Hong Kong) in 1910. Ryan was the last person of the group to leave Japan, in the fall of 1910. (*ibid*, p. 32)

Before and after Ryan's group left Japan, other Pentecostal missionaries came to Japan one after another. (Suzuki, 2001a) Before the establishment of the General Council of the Assemblies of God in 1914, all of those who came were lay missionaries. The missionaries were in contact with each other and gradually formed a Pentecostal group in Japan.

The most influential missionaries to whom we can trace the roots of the Japan Assemblies of God are the Juergensen family members. The ministry of the Juergensen family influenced the pre-history of Japan Assemblies of God. Carl Fredrick Juergensen (1862-1940) and his family (his wife and two daughters) arrived in Japan in August of 1913. They began to minister at Hongo and Kamifujimae in Tokyo. One year after the Juergensen's arrival, the General Council of the Assemblies of God was established in the U.S. "C. F. Juergensen was officially appointed an AoG missionary on May 23, 1918." (Shew, 2002:42) He served in Japan for 27 years until his death at the age of 77. After 1919, more official Assembly of God missionaries began to come to Japan. One of them was J. W. Juergensen, the son of C. F. Juergensen.

The ministry of the Juergensen family advanced due to their encounter with Kiyoma Yumiyama. Kiyoma Yumiyama

(1900-2002) became a Christian at the age of 21 when he was a student at a medical college in Okayama. (Takaguchi, 2002) He felt God's calling to be a minister. He abandoned the idea of becoming a doctor and dropped out of school when he was 23 years old. He went to Tokyo and started an independent ministry there. At the end of 1922, Yumiyama attended a Pentecostal meeting and there met John W. Juergensen.[1] Yumiyama immediately felt the importance of the Pentecostal message and began to seek after the experience of baptism in the Holy Spirit. As a result, he was baptized in the Spirit accompanied by speaking in tongues and joined John's ministry at the beginning of 1923.

At church, Yumiyama helped with the ministries of printing, Bible school, and evangelism. (Nihon Assenburiizu obu Goddo Kyodan, 1989:202) He studied the Bible with John Juergensen every day.

In April of 1924, C. F. Juergensen and his family came back to Japan. John and his wife moved to Akabane, and Yumiyama became a Japanese mission worker and began to help with Carl Frederick Juergensen's ministries. In 1927, Carl Juergensen built a church at Takinogawa (this was the oldest Pentecostal church building in Japan) and appointed Yumiyama to be the pastor in March 1928. (Shinsho Kirisuto Kyokai, 2002:21)

This Pentecostal group called themselves the Japan Bible Church (Nihon Seisho Kyokai). The number of local churches increased, and native leaders slowly but surely began to join the

---

[1]See (Nihon Assenburiizu obu Goddo Kyodan Rekishi Hensan Iinkai, 1999:54) C. F. Juergensen was in the U.S. on furlough at that time.

group. The following table lists the growth of the churches and their membership at that time. [2]

Year	Churches	Members
1929	7	126
1930	8	157
1933	20	292

In 1937 C.F. Juergensen and Yumiyama left the Japan Bible Church. They founded Takinogawa Holy Spirit Church (*Takinogawa Seirei Kyokai*) in 1938. The leaders of this group were C. F. Juergensen and his daughter Marie, and Japanese leader Kiyoma Yumiyama. The leaders of Japan Bible Church were Barth and Byers who came to Japan in 1927, and the Japanese leader was Jun Murai. Japan Bible Church had 15 churches and Takinogawa had 4 churches at that time. (Shew, 2003:376)

Interestingly, Juergensen's son John continued to participate with the Japan Bible Church organization rather than with Takinogawa.

After that, Japanese Pentecostal churches followed two roads until the establishment of the Japan AoG in 1949.

Japan Bible Church

Year	Churches	Members
1938	20	262
1939	20	326

Takinogawa

Year	Churches	Members
1939	6	Unknown

[2] The number of churches and members are from *Nihon Kirisutokyo Nenkan [Japan Christianity Yearbook]*.

Just before World War II, the relationship between Japan and Western countries became strained and the wartime government exerted more pressure on the Christian churches. Before the Pacific War occurred, almost all foreign missionaries had to leave Japan on the orders of the government. Even missionaries from both Japan Bible Church and Takinogawa Holy Spirit Church, such as Barth, Byers, Marie and Agnes Juergensen, went back to their home countries in 1941. Byers and Marie Juergensen came back to Japan after the war.

In 1941, the Japan Bible Church encountered a theological problem. Murai and his colleagues were invited by the True Jesus Church to minister in Taiwan for one month (Taiwan was part of the Japanese Empire between 1895 and 1945). However, the True Jesus Church was Oneness Pentecostal. During the trip, Murai accepted the teaching of the True Jesus Church and left the Japan Bible Church. (Nihon Assenburiizu obu Goddo Kyodan Rekishi Hensan Iinkai, 1999:61) He then founded a new denomination, named the Spirit of Jesus Church (*Iesu no Mitama Kyokai*).

The wartime government forced all of the Protestant churches to join one denomination so they could be easily controlled. Both the remaining flocks of the Japan Bible Church and Yumiyama's Takinogawa Holy Spirit Church joined the United Church of Christ in Japan (Nihon Kirisuto Kyodan) in 1941. During the war, Christian pastors all underwent severe hardship. They were repeatedly persecuted by the government. In addition, some pastors were forced to join the army and go into battle. The churches that could continue meeting were very few.

After the war, Christians finally received the freedom to evangelise. Many missionaries who were forced to leave Japan came back again. The Japanese Pentecostal ministers who were forced to join the United Church of Christ in Japan did not want to remain in it any more, and began to desire to establish a new Pentecostal group. In 1946, Kenko Ohchi and Tsuru Nagashima, who were ministers with the Japan Bible Church, tried to mediate between Yumiyama, the leader of Takinogawa, (Tokyo) and Hajime Kawasaki, who was a pastor in the Japan Bible Church. Yumiyama and Kawasaki met and decided to establish a new Pentecostal denomination together.

After several meetings, they finally founded the Japan Assemblies of God (*Nihon Assenburiizu obu Goddo Kyodan*) on March 15, 1949. At the first conference, there were 19 people in attendance: 7 missionaries and 12 Japanese ministers. There were 13 churches with a total membership of about 800.[3] Yumiyama was chosen as the general superintendent. Yumiyama led the Japan AoG in this role for 25 years, until 1973.

Other Pentecostal missionaries arrived in Japan one after another and formed their own Pentecostal groups. For instance, missionaries from the Open Bible and Foursquare churches arrived in Japan in 1950. (Kurisuchan Shimbun, 2003:605, 615) Not only Western missionaries but also Korean ministers brought the Pentecostal message. Jashil Choi, mother-in-law of Cho Yonggi, started ministry in Japan around 1971. (She was ordained by the Japan Assemblies of God in 1972.) (Senoo, 2001:137) In 1977, Cho Yonggi led a revival meeting with Jashil Choi. From that time until now, Cho has frequently come to Japan to work for "the salvation of

[3]See Nihon Assenburiizu obu Goddo Kyodan Rekishi Hensan Iinkai 1999:85. However, according to Yumiyama (1977:64), the members were at most 300.

10 million Japanese [*Issenman Kyurei*]." Some members of the Yoido Full Gospel Church in Tokyo started a meeting which grew rapidly, and in 1979 the Full Gospel Church in Japan was established.

At present, there are many Pentecostal organizations in Japan. While the mainline Protestant churches seem to be struggling with mission in Japan, we can say that comparatively speaking the Pentecostal churches are increasing in numbers and in membership.

Figure 4.1: Rate of Church Growth in Japan (1984-1988) (Ogata, 1997:272)

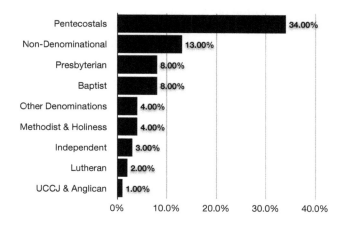

The chart above shows the rate of church growth in Japan from 1984 to 1988. We can see how the Pentecostal churches are growing the fastest in Japan. According to Fukuda, when this chart was made (1989), only 7% of all the Protestant churches (5700) were Pentecostal/Charismatics. And yet, the rate of growth of the Pentecostals—34%—is the most among all the Protestant churches. (Fukuda, 1992:212) While most of the churches grew at a rate of less than 10%, the growth of the Pentecostal churches has been, by comparison, surprisingly large.

Next, let us examine each Pentecostal group. The table opposite compares the chief Pentecostal churches in 1964 and 2004.[4]

In 1998, the Japan Assemblies of God called together some of the main Pentecostal groups in Japan and formed the Japan Pentecostal Council. (Nihon Assenburiizu obu Goddo Kyodan Rekishi Hensan Iinkai, 1999:225) The purpose of this conference is "to promote the sound growth of the Pentecostal faith in Japan." (Yoshiyama, 2001:97) The members are the Japan Assemblies of God, Japan Open Bible, Japan Church of God, Japan Foursquare, Zion Mission, Japan Pentecostal Church, The Family of God, Calvary Christ, The Fellowship of Independent Pentecostal Church and Japan Next Towns Mission. (*ibid*, p. 97) The general superintendent of the Japan AoG serves as the chairman and periodic conferences are held.

4.2 Mission Strategies of the Pentecostal Churches

One predominant mission strategy of the Pentecostals has been tent meeting evangelism (*Ten-maku dendo*). (Nihon Assenburiizu obu Goddo Kyodan Rekishi Hensan Iinkai,

---

[4]Figures quoted from the Christian Year Book, 1964 and 2004 editions.

	Churches in 1964	Members in 1964	Churches in 2004	Members in 2004
Japan Assemblies of God	115	4,002	209	13,525
Japan Open Bible	8	444	16	1,203
Japan Church of God	5	55	9	450
Japan Foursquare Gospel	3	72	26	1,079
Japan Pentecost	10	358	20	919
Family of God Christian Church			9	553
The Fellowship of Independent Pentecostal Churches			70	2,180
Japan Full Gospel Association			65	6,238
The Flock of the Gospel of Jesus Christ			18	753
Next Towns Mission in Japan			21	940

1999:57, 59) This strategy was often seen before and after the War. The missionaries found a vacant lot, pitched a tent, and held evangelical meetings. To gather people, they stood by the roadside and made appeals (*robo dendo*). The usual approach to *robo dendo* was to sing some hymns with a drum, a bell, or a trumpet, and to preach. In the past, many people gathered immediately in response and followed the missionaries to the tent. If some people were saved as a result of the tent meeting, a church would form. This style of the mission was continued by even national ministers. (See *ibid*, pp. 59, 74)

As Japan grew financially, and the society became sophisticated in the post-war era, the style of the tent meeting evangelism disappeared because it became difficult to find vacant lots for evangelism. However, the spirit of church planting still remains. As we can see from the previous table, Pentecostal local churches are rapidly increasing.

Church planting is definitely one of the characteristics of the Pentecostal mission strategies. Japan Assemblies of God in particular respects the value of training ministers and sends many graduates to carry out church planting. As an epoch-making mission strategy, in the 1985 general meeting, Japan Assemblies of God resolved that they would grow from 142 to 250 churches by 1999. (Nihon Assenburiizu obu Goddo Kyodan Rekishi Hensan Iinkai, 1999:166) Although this aim was not exactly achieved, this project promoted Pentecostal missions in Japan. Japan Assemblies of God has 210 churches and about 13,500 members at present.[5]

Mass evangelism is also one particular mission strategy of the Pentecostal church. (Nihon Assenburiizu obu Goddo

[5]Figures taken from the 2004 annual general meeting of Japan Assemblies of God.

Kyodan Rekishi Hensan Iinkai, 1999:114) After the war, Japan experienced rapid urbanization. As people moved to big cities from the countryside, they became comparatively disconnected from traditional customs such as Buddhist and Shinto rituals as opposed to the lifestyle they had in their hometowns. Even now, Evangelical churches work together for mission campaigns targeting city dwellers. They use big concert halls or even baseball stadiums and promote the meetings with the help of extensive financial support. The Pentecostal churches often join this kind of crusade-style meetings; for instance, Japan Assemblies of God has joined the administration of the Billy Graham Christian Crusade. (*ibid*, p. 220)

What is more, healing crusades are a characteristic of the Pentecostal Charismatic style of mass evangelism. For instance, in 1960, Japan Assemblies of God invited Oral Roberts to Japan. (*ibid*, p. 117) Nowadays healing crusades are held by the Charismatic camp and the Third Wave movement.

4.3 Pentecostal Mission Strategy: Its Strengths and Weaknesses

The eagerness for evangelism appears to be the strongest side of the Pentecostal church. Church leaders always emphasize the need for mission and encourage their members to share the Gospel with their families and friends. The Pentecostals' aggressive church planting is a particularly remarkable movement in Japanese Christianity. One cannot but admire the efforts of those ministers who boldly go to unknown places and try to build up the Body of Christ.

The message of blessing that the Pentecostals originally proclaimed seems to be another strength of their message. As mentioned in the previous chapter, ordinary Japanese have the impression that Christianity is a knowledge-centered religion. On the one hand, the Japanese religious mind is blessing (*goriyaku*)-centered, while on the other hand, the Christian church primarily emphasizes the spiritual life, and thus creates a distance between the spiritual and the human desires of this world. The Pentecostal message of blessing can help people grasp the meaning of the Christian faith.

What is more, the experiential message, including healing, stressed by Pentecostals, is also a positive and effective strategy for mission in Japan. Fukuda examines the reason for the growth of Pentecostals, and points out that the healing ministry of Pentecostals seems to meet the needs of Japanese. (Fukuda, 1992:213) While the first Japanese Christians were mainly from the upper class who were attracted by the Christian message of new knowledge and new morals, ordinary Japanese were not interested in the Christian message as much as these upper classes. For the majority of Japanese, religious experience is more important than knowledge and morality. Not only healing but also other biblical experiences, such as the baptism in the Holy Spirit and speaking in tongues, can be a powerful bridge between Christianity and the Japanese people.

When it comes to weaknesses, however, it seems that the mission strategy of tent evangelism or mass evangelistic meetings is rather out-of-date. When Japan was in poverty and social upheaval following the War, Japanese people were seeking something new (and in a sense, something American) and were drawn into Christian churches. The tent meeting and evangelistic meeting (crusade) style of evangelism practiced by the Pentecostals in the past certainly did attract people. After Japan became financially stable, however, many people lost interest in Christianity. Nowadays, in my experience, if the church plans an evangelistic meeting, there will be few newcomers who come simply because they received information about the meeting. People have many attractive choices for things to do on Sunday morning. It is very difficult for Japanese people to come to church for the first time without having specific reason.

Secondly, it seems that Japanese Pentecostal churches are relatively unconcerned about social needs of their local communities, although they insist on preaching the Gospel. Since many churches do not have much contact with their local communities, they are isolated from their communities. This attitude may cause people to think that Christianity is irrelevant to them and thus hinder them in going to church. In order to develop contact with its local community, the local church should do something that meets the felt needs of that community.

Thirdly, the structure of the Church seems to agitate against mission work by lay believers. As stated in the previous chapter, one of the problems of Japanese churches is their clergy-centered structure. Even Pentecostal churches seem to suffer from this tendency. Needless to say, the empowerment of lay people is one of the characteristics and strengths of the Pentecostal message. Unfortunately, however, it seems that the clergy-centered mind prevails even within the Japanese Pentecostal churches and prevents the laity from ministering freely and actively. The members have to ask their pastors what they should do, and they do what their pastors tell them to do. This kind of attitude is deeply rooted in Japanese churches. The Pentecostal church should encourage and help its members to exercise their gifts effectively.

Fourthly, it seems that the Japanese Pentecostal church lacks a theoretical basis for its mission strategy that includes contextualization, makes good use of the Pentecostal distinctives, and takes into account the basic patterns of Japanese religion and society. Japanese churches, including the Pentecostals, tend to follow and maintain the teachings of missionaries. This is not always a bad thing, but sometimes it means that a Japanese church is primarily Western or American in its forms and mindset, which in turn means that ordinary Japanese people cannot accept it as a religion for them. In other words, it is necessary that native Japanese ministers theologize Japanese culture, religious traditions, and the Japanese mindset, and pursue unique mission strategies that are not imported from other countries.

Chapter 5

Suggested Pentecostal Mission Strategies

In the second chapter, I examined the Japanese worldview, including their religious thinking. In the third and the fourth chapter, I dealt with the history and the mission strategies of the Japanese churches. In this last chapter, I would like to discuss what can be done to evangelize unreached Japanese souls. Especially as a Pentecostal, I would like to argue how we can extract distinctive Pentecostal strengths and utilize them in support of our strategy.

5.1 Improper Approaches to Japanese

First of all, in reviewing the arguments of the preceding chapters, let us think about some reasons why the mission strategies of the church have not been as successful in gaining the lost as expected. There seem to have been several improper approaches to reaching out to the Japanese. I would like to present three major problems.

5.1.1   The Concept of an Absolute

One of the biggest reasons why many Japanese cannot accept Biblical truth is that there is no concept of absoluteness in the Japanese mindset. Japanese have historically recognised new religious truths without denying their former faith(s). When Buddhism was introduced to Japan in the sixth century A.D., Japanese did not deny their original Shinto but skillfully made the two religions compatible. In the same way, Japanese accepted Confucianism and other philosophical systems from China. Japan even granted Western civilization entrance after the opening of the country in the 19th century. The Japanese succeeded in acquiring foreign forms, without necessarily grasping even a fraction of their underlying values. In effect, since Japanese do not possess the concept of absoluteness, they can easily import foreign thoughts and sometimes even change them into suitable ones for the Japanese. (Oyama, 1995:89)

When I was a Bible college student, I often heard that we had to teach the concepts of God, sin, and salvation to the unreached Japanese first of all. It meant that we had to give them the absolute truth of Christianity. First, we had to tell them that there is only one God who has created the heavens and the earth. As many senior pastors told us, then we were to teach the concept of sin and salvation. Yet it seems that these concepts do not necessarily have an effect on the Japanese when they encounter the Gospel. Japanese cannot understand the basics of the Biblical faith because they are polytheists and tend to deny absolute existence. "For Japanese, such belief that God is only one is not 'truth', at least not meaningful truth, no matter how veritable this belief may be." (Nagasawa, 2002) If we insist on absolute Christian concepts to Japanese at first, we may find that many people become agitated or cannot accept the concept. This is not to say that Japanese do not nor cannot believe the Biblical faith, but that they just cannot accept many of its concepts initially. At the same time, I am not saying that it is not necessary to teach the absoluteness of Christianity; needless to say, it is imperative to fix Biblical truth as absolute truth in Christians' minds. What I would like to say is that if we consider the concept of absoluteness as the entranceway to Christianity for Japanese people, we may well find that this entrance point to the Christian faith is too narrow for ordinary Japanese to enter.

It may be better to realise that it takes time for Japanese to understand the Biblical faith because of their existent viewpoint, and so it may not be wise to insist that Japanese believe in Biblical truths such as the absoluteness and uniqueness of God, such as original sin, and such as the notion of salvation, at the very first stage of evangelistic encounter. Even if many Japanese will not accept belief in Jesus Christ as their own Savior as a first step, it may just be because they are confused by their pre-existing worldview. If we conclude that because of that they are rejecting the truth, we run the risk of abandoning contact with them from that point on.

It is essential to assume it takes time for a Japanese person to fully understand Biblical truth, and if we accept this, it might be good to allow Japanese to go through the gateway of Christian fellowship first, and give them Biblical truth step-by-step through their experience in church.

5.1.2 Intellectual Approach

As stated before, Japanese by nature receive religious truth primarily through experience, such as by participating in ritual, and yet many Japanese think of Christianity as a knowledge-centered religion. We accept that Biblical truth based on knowledge is very important for Japanese Christians who live in a pagan society like Japan; however, if we present the Gospel as no more than knowledge, we will notice that many Japanese do not have interest in such a gospel. Makito Nagasawa, a Japanese minister who is currently working in Mongolia, makes the following suggestion for reaching Japanese:

> In the Japanese context, truth is experiential and personal. Truth as philosophical or conceptual, separated from feeling, is almost meaningless to the Japanese. Thus they are looking for communities in which spiritual experiences are tangible and real. We have to start with personal experience.(Nagasawa, 2002)

As he says, it is vital that we introduce a Gospel that can be experienced.

Did Jesus preach a Gospel of mere knowledge? He healed many people and did many miracles, and the people regarded what Jesus himself did as the Good News. When the disciples of John the Baptist asked Jesus who Jesus was,

> Jesus answered and said to them, "Go and tell John the things you have seen and heard: that the blind see, the lame walk, the lepers are cleansed, the deaf hear, the dead are raised, the poor have the gospel preached to them." (Luke 7:22 NKJ)

The ministry of Jesus was total and was accompanied by something visible and tangible. In other words, it was something that humans could experience. Therefore, if we present the gospel as something which we can experience, we may be able to see people becoming interested in it.

Pentecostal ministries have an advantage in this matter. They can preach the Gospel by proclaiming the experience and the work of the Holy Spirit. The Gospel that we preach must involve the experience of the Biblical truth so that people will know that the Christian faith is not merely *knowing* but is also *experiencing*.

Healing ministry should be holistic. People are seeking healing not only of their bodies but also of mind and spirit. Jesus Christ can touch the whole human. We need to introduce Jesus Christ not as knowledge but as personality and power.

5.1.3 Disregarding the Group-Oriented Nature of Japanese

The last inadequate mission approach is asking or demanding people to leave the community to which they belong. The Japanese are a group-oriented people, as mentioned in the second chapter. They fear being isolated from their communities of family, school, and work place. On the contrary, perhaps unconsciously, it seems that the traditional mission approach of the Christian church is to encourage people to move away from their communities. "In Japan, people do not act according to the standard that they regard as right. They always watch other people and think that it is better to do what other people do." (Oyama, 1995:103) For the people who are not in Christian homes, they cannot imagine being a Christian, not because they deny the Christian faith, but because they are unable to leave their community, especially their families. "In fact, membership in Japanese religious organizations has typically been by families and not by individuals." (Boyle, 1986:67)

One Japanese pastor points out that "it is necessary for Japanese to have one more decision other than the decision to believe in the Gospel. This is the decision to join the church. This is one more difficult and crucial phase."(Goto, 2002:216) For Japanese, it is vital to consider whether or not it is worth belonging to the church. In other words, a local church should be a community which gives comfort and is easy to join. It does not make sense for us to make the unchurched afraid of cutting off their former lives before they have discovered that the church can be a replacement community. Unless church provides the unchurched with a safe and a comfortable community to which to belong, we will not see people willing to enter the church.

Over all, these approaches give the impression of individualism, of Western ideas, and of ignoring human relationships. In addition, these approaches do not fit Japanese religious thinking in terms of belonging to a community, religious experience, and daily benefit.

5.2   Process of Paradigm Shift

Next, I would like to discuss how we can overcome these improper approaches to mission in Japan, and how we invite the lost into the Kingdom of God.   As we have seen, conventional mission approaches do not seem to work effectively. It is clear that we need a paradigm shift in evangelism.

Here, I would like to suggest some paradigm shifts.

5.2.1 Paradigm Shift

The fundamental mistake seems to spring from false premises; we have believed that we have to make people go through the following process in order to become saved:

To hear → To understand → To believe

This means that we have tried to lead people into hearing the Gospel first, understanding it second, and then believing in. Yet, if we try to push people through this procedure, we must first force them to accept absolute truth at the first stage of becoming Christians. This approach is knowledge-centered and does not consider the fear of being isolated from community.

In other words, this approach is quite individualistic. Even if it works in Western culture and society, it does not always work in a traditionally group-oriented culture such as Japan.

My suggestion is that the process for a Japanese person to become a Christian should be as follows:

To belong → To experience → To believe

For many Japanese, accepting a faith means belonging to some community. While Westerners find their identity in their belief, Japanese find their identity in the place to which they are attached. Unless they find a place in which to belong, they cannot fully think about faith. Besides this, unless they feel that they are accepted, they will never open their hearts. Experience is therefore particularly crucial in Japanese religious thinking. Japanese cannot grasp a sense of faith until they experience something of the religious. So, we should change our paradigm and try to bring people into the community of Christ first.

Next, let us think about the type of places to which we bring people. We might have had a premise about evangelism up until now, that is, an assumption that we must bring people into a church—one might say that it represents "a place of God's control"—and yet, there are high emotional walls for Japanese to climb over in order to enter a church.

If we regard evangelism as a one-time event, we will lose many souls. As previously mentioned, it is not that Japanese do not want to believe in Christ, but they need some time to overcome their pre-existing worldview. If we push them to decide right away, many of them cannot do so and both we and they have to give up.

To solve this problem, let us consider the concept of "a pre-church"; we could say that this represents "a place of God's influence." People cannot be a member of God's Kingdom unless they confess that Christ is the Lord. And yet, the Holy Spirit can influence even those who are not yet involved in a church. Jesus mixed with many people who did not even know who He was. He ate meals with those who were ignored,

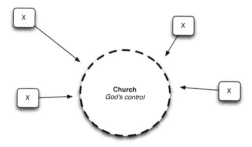

Figure 5.1: X = an individual. We try to make people come to church, but there are high walls around the church.

discriminated against, and regarded as sinners. He simply plunged into the crowd.

In doing so, Jesus healed and liberated many who were suffering from sicknesses and evil spirits. We can see in the book of Acts that Jesus' disciples could do the same things by the power of the Holy Spirit. All could be influenced, touched and led by the Spirit, even when they did not belong to the Christian church.

Our aim is thus to bring our Christian fellowship out of the church and to receive the unchurched into it. In the fellowship, the first priority, even before preaching the Gospel, is to develop human relationships. We should understand people before demanding that they understand us. At the same time, we also expect the Holy Spirit to lead us and to act powerfully within the spiritual community.

Within the field of God's influence, people can take time to think about the Christian faith without any pressure, and

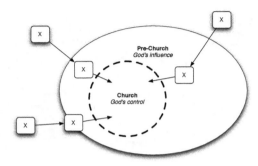

Figure 5.2: An individual can be led into pre-church and then into the Church.

we can then encourage people to decide to follow Jesus Christ and to become a member of the body of Christ. Needless to say, we have to extend the realm of God's influence as much as we can so that many people have the opportunity to experience fellowship.

5.3   In the Spiritual Community

Let us now think about how next to lead the unchurched further into the fellowship of God.

5.3.1   Fellowship with love

In the field of God's influence, first of all, we should expect that people will see a spiritual community where people can be open and feel accepted and loved.

Mitsuo Fukuda, a missiologist, points out that "in the Japanese context, the most functional approach to mission and pastoral ministry will prioritize human relationships."(Fukuda, 1992:216) I agree with this idea. Before we preach the Gospel, we should hear the voice of the people and develop human relationships with them. We invite people to come into fellowship with us. In all honestly, people are seeking a place where they can feel befriended, loved, and accepted. We should aim to show the presence of God's love from the outset.

If we can present the Christian community by showing them how we love, help, and serve each other, we can remove their fear and prejudice, and encourage them to join the community in which the Holy Spirit reigns. The most important point is that we should present communities that meet the needs of the unchurched Japanese people.

From there, how do we accept people into our fellowship? I would like to conclude that we Pentecostals should be more involved in ministry that helps those who with specific needs, just as Jesus and the disciples did. This is the task of those who are given the Spirit. We may call that our holistic ministry.

Although Japan seems to be a sophisticated and relatively wealthy country, there are many serious social problems, just as there are in other countries. It is not unreasonable to say that many of the problems are based on the fundamental problem of human relationships: many people are suffering from broken relationships with others. I believe that we can and should help them to restore their injured hearts and minds.

I would like to produce some examples for bringing people into our fellowship. For instance, what about a free church school? One of the biggest social problems in Japan is *Fu-Toko*, when children stop going to school.[1] It is thought that the biggest reason for this is that they cannot maintain sound relationships with others. They do not work nor help their parents but simply stay at home. According to statistics from the Ministry of Education, Culture, Sports, Science, and Technology, there were more than 123,000 children who did not go to school last year.[3] This is a serious problem in Japan. This is not only a problem for children, but is also a problem for their parents.

Some churches have begun to minister to this problem. For those children who cannot go to school, church offers the opportunity to study at the church. In the church, the children are touched by the love of Christ and taught Biblical truth. It is reported that many children's lives are restored, and they come to accept Jesus through the church school ministry. (Kurisuchan Shimbun [The Christian Newspaper], 2001)

There are some other aspects with which we can help those who are in trouble within Japanese society. Rapid urbanization has increased the number of nuclear families. Nowadays, many young parents (especially mothers) are struggling with parenting. They do not know how to deal with their children. This is also a problem of human relationship. It

---

[1] This term indicates only students of compulsory education (elementary school and junior high school). But there are more people (over 15 years old) who cannot maintain adequate contact with others and who do not leave their homes for a long time, sometimes years. This is called *hikikomori*, or social phobia. It is said that there are over one million people with this problem.[2]

[3] Ministry of Education, Culture, Sports, Science and Technology Japan, *Fundamental Statistics About School Education*, Japanese, http://www.mext.go.jp/b_menu/toukei/001/04073001/001.htm, 22 August, 2005.

is crucial for churches to organize fellowship for these young mothers so that they can share their problems and find some solutions.

Japan is experiencing a major problem that few other countries have seen before: the rapid development of an aging society. According to the report by the Ministry of Health and Welfare, (2005) in 2003, 19.0% of Japan's population were more than 65 years of age. This means one in five Japanese is older than 65 years old. The government further predicts that in 2015, the percentage of 65 year old citizens will be 26.0%. That is, more than one in *four* Japanese will be older than 65 years old. What is more, the report states two more points: first, the elderly tend to live in cities rather than in the countryside; and second, the proportion of elderly who live alone is increasing. Can we approach such people with the ministry of our fellowship?

Next, how about a gospel choir school? Today many Japanese like to sing gospel music. Black Gospel music is especially popular. Recently, through gospel choir schools, many people (especially young women) are being saved. (Ribaibaru Shimbun [The Revival Times], 2003b)

The overall point is that we have to form channels to communicate with non-believers and help them become part of our church activities.

5.3.2   Experience of the Holy Spirit

Then, in the fellowship, we expect that people will experience something spiritual. We express ourselves to one another, and even share together our problems and needs. We minister

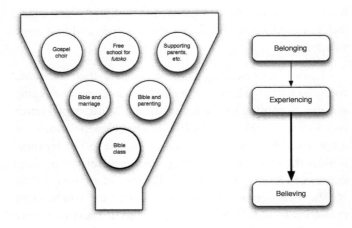

Figure 5.3: The Paradigm Shift: A New Process of Becoming a Christian (See Ribaibaru Shimbun [The Revival Times] 2003a)

to each other and pray for one another. When we have a fellowship filled with the Spirit, we can anticipate that even non-believers will feel the power of God.

Blessing can be a powerful message. The Japanese church has tended to emphasize only notional domains such as eternal life and deliverance from sin and not much on specific living needs. As previously stated, however, people long for worldly benefits such as health, financial success, and religious protection from evil from religion. When they find that God can answer their requests, they will have contact with the God of Christianity. We should expect that the Holy Spirit will meet their physical, emotional, and spiritual needs.

Needless to say, a power encounter is one of the effective

points that non-believers can experience. Even in Japan, a sophisticated and high technology society, many people are consciously or unconsciously aware of spiritual reality. "The appearance of new religions which emphasize healing, miracles, ancestor worship, spells, and good or evil genius, and the boom of fortune telling, occult, and New-age movement show the Japanese original worldview." (Ogata, 1997:310) In the depth of their minds, people believe in invisible spiritual power. We should expect that people will see that Christian faith has spiritual power.

Satyavrata claims that "a personal experience of the Spirit is undeniably the central focus of Pentecostal spirituality." Even for Japanese, being touched by God will be a big turning point in their lives.

5.3.3 Accepting the Truth

The next stage is the truth encounter. When they realize that they are accepted and loved, and have experienced God's work, they finally are ready to be taught Biblical truth. It is important to open the Bible together and help them to understand the truth step by step.

In this point, I would like to suggest that we should begin with what is relevant to their needs. What are their problems in life? Do they have a problem in their marriage, in their interpersonal relationships, or with their children? We focus on what they need or what they want to know.

Then, let us connect these problems with the Bible. In general, Japanese respect the Bible, even if they have a negative image of Christianity and the Church. Ordinary Japanese know that the Bible is the oldest sacred book, and it has produced many cultures, great arts, and life teachings. We can show that there are answers to our life problems in the Bible. For instance, in our church we hold a number of Bible classes, with titles such as "The Bible and Marriage," "The Bible and Success," "The Bible and Family," and "The Bible and Child Raising." These courses have at least three series. We have a meal time, testimonies, prayer, and we find applications of these topics from the Bible. Little by little, the people come to know what a Christian is. The purpose is to open the hearts of those who have problems and to examine their real life situations.

My other suggestion is that we should encourage them to do something specific that the Bible says in their daily lives. We should not make the Word of God just a book of knowledge. Makito Nagasawa proposes that "it is more appropriate for the Japanese to define the Bible as the canon designed for teaching which is to be practiced, rather than teaching which is to be accepted as beliefs." (Nagasawa, 2002:59) Non-believers need to realize that when they put the Word of God into practice, they will experience God's love and power and be blessed.

For some, it may be forgiveness. For others, it may be reconciliation. It may be the abandonment of selfishness. There are many teachings in the Bible that challenge the Japanese worldview. Experiencing God's word in their daily lives, Japanese can recognize what they should follow.

Then, we introduce them to the person of Jesus Christ. We do not lead them into a religion, but to Jesus Himself. If they become aware of Jesus and the power of the Christian life, they may pursue deeper questions about the purpose of their lives. Our aim is to help them to discover how Jesus can be concerned with them in the specific situations they find themselves. We tell them why we need Jesus, how Jesus saves us, where Jesus brings us, and what Jesus expects us to do, as well as other basic teachings. It goes without saying that we should expect the Holy Spirit who points to the cross of Jesus Christ to lead them into the full presence of God during the sharing of the Word.

5.3.4 Modelling of Lifestyle

Lastly, we should conclude this process by modelling a powerful Christian life. "In the context of fellowship with Christians, they will see a living example of the new life and how it works." (*ibid*, p. 61) To be honest, many Japanese are looking for a visible model to follow. Many people are oppressed with anxiety about such things as the future, family, finances, human relationships, low self-esteem, and addictions. Who can be released from this suffering? If the Christians can show the unchurched how they live in freedom in this world, can show the difference between a Christian and a non-Christian, and can show that Christians have astonishing power to live, unreached people will naturally desire to be like them. They will follow a model Christian who is fully alive and who deals with actual problems, and finally they will find out the key to that person's walk. If they realize that faith in Christ Jesus is the key, they will decide to follow Him. This is the moment of believing and becoming a member of the Church.

As pointed out again and again, it is difficult for Japanese to immediately take large steps toward an unknown realm. Human relationships may help them move toward the Christian faith step by step.

As we have seen, we need to change the paradigm of our evangelism. We need to bring our fellowship out of the church and receive the unreached people into that fellowship so that they can feel loved and accepted at first. To win the Japanese we have to have many channels that they can freely and easily join and which help them feel that they belong. After that, we have to effectively present the Word of God to them. It must begin with their essential problems or needs. Attending a church service should come after they believe in Jesus.

The most important point is reliance upon the Holy Spirit. "There are no rules and regulations for mission, because Spirit leadership is central." (Pinnock, 1996:145) Only the Holy Spirit knows the needs of the lost and can touch their lives. The Bible tells us that God has set eternity in human hearts (Ecclesiastes 3:11). Even Japanese have a longing for this kind of spiritual eternity. It is imperative that we do not overstep the authority of the Spirit. We have to obey the guidance of the Spirit so that the Spirit freely works among the unreached.

5.4   Toward a Spiritual Community

It is clear that the suggested mission strategy that I have written about here is not the task of the pastor alone. This must be a team ministry. The members' fellowship itself must be the spiritual community that attracts the unreached people. I would dare to say that all Christians should be evangelists by the empowerment of the Holy Spirit and form a community filled with the Holy Spirit.

In this last section, let us consider how we equip ourselves for the task of mission in Japan and how we develop a spiritual community where the Spirit freely works on behalf of the lost.

5.4.1 Cultivating the Members

Many ministers who work in Japan point out that the Japanese church is clergy-centered. (See, e.g. Furuya 2003:27, Nicolas 2003:234, Ogata 1997:305 It seems that even the Pentecostal church is influenced by this tradition. Pastors appear to do everything and lay members merely follow the pastors' instructions.

This does not mean that every aspect of the Japanese church is bad, but to see a great spiritual awakening in Japan, we will have to raise up a lay movement. Ogata points out that one of the keys for the rapid growth of new religions in Japan is their system of lay believers' activities. (Ogata, 1997:294) Soka Gakkai, one of the influential new religions which arose out of Buddhist teaching, has grown mainly through small group activity in the believers' houses. (*Ibid.*, p. 302) This indicates that small group evangelism and lay leadership training have the potential possibility of fulfilling God's mission in Japan.

The mission of the minister is to "prepare God's people for works of service, so that the body of Christ may be built up" (Eph. 4:12 [NIV]). We Pentecostals especially believe and emphasize that the Holy Spirit empowers every believer to witness. We should demonstrate how Christians achieve spiritual empowerment for the mission of the church.

To accomplish this vocation, I would like to propose that the clergy-centered structure of the church needs to be revised from the bottom up. The Holy Spirit makes us one body so that we share spiritual gifts with each other and take care of one another (1 Corinthians 12). The duty of the pastor is very important, but at the same time, other gifts that the members

have been given should also be regarded as vital. When all
the members freely exercise their gifts and continually focus
on reaching out to the lost who are outside the church, the
church will become a true spiritual community and draw in
the unchurched who are searching for a real place to which
they can belong.

5.4.2   Proper Training

Needless to say, every Christian should be trained to serve and
build up the body of Christ. Unfortunately, however, statistics
show that the lifetime of a Japanese Christian is 2.8 years.
(Furuya, 2003:105–106) This means that many converts leave
the church within less than three years after being baptized.
We have to conclude that we are not effectively making new
believers true disciples of Christ, and that our training has not
been adequate for those who become Christians in Japan.

It seems that many local churches regard discipleship
training as just a Bible study. Equipping members should not
be just a Bible class. Of course, knowledge of Christian belief
is certainly very significant in order to live as Christians, but
at the same time, converts need to know some more specific
modes of operation in order to deal with their daily situations.
In other words, they need to practice connecting their faith
with their lives. Training should be specific and practical.

We also need to train the members to be leaders of small
groups and to be evangelists. From the very beginning of
Christian life, believers must be taught that they have to be
the ones who lead others to Christ and equip them for the
Kingdom of God.

5.4.3   Delegating a Proper Field of Ministry

Ministers should positively delegate particular fields of ministry to the members.   Unless Christians have a proper situation in which they can exercise their gifts, their training will not be effective.

The most important point is that pastors delegate their tasks to their members. A pastor needs to assign the leadership of small groups, Bible classes, and evangelical activities to the members. Delegation may carry some risk and bring anxiety to pastors or sometimes even cause confusion in the church. If a local church, however, aims to be an effective missional church in the community, it must inevitably challenge the members to take on the task of mission.

One of the characteristics of the early Pentecostal movement was the spontaneity of the lay members.   Once they experienced the baptism in the Holy Spirit, they boldly became missionaries and went out into their communities. Even within a local church, we should encourage the members to become themselves ministers filled with the Spirit and we therefore should offer them opportunities for ministry.

5.4.4   Creating the Proper Strategy

It seems that we Pentecostals have so far encouraged the members to just preach the Gospel and have not thought about or taught a specific strategy. However, as previously discussed, to communicate with unchurched people, we have to find effective means to suit our ends. This does not mean that we do not need the guidance of the Holy Spirit. On the contrary, we have to totally depend on the Spirit. And yet, depending on the Spirit does not mean that all we have to do is to pray. We should seek for wisdom from the Spirit while being conscious of the people that we are targeting. As Fukuda says,

> it seems that investigative research is one of the most neglected processes in Japan. Christian communicators need to understand the people to whom they are delivering the Gospel. If they engage in the study of finances, worldviews, politics, work situations, and the religion of the recipients of the Gospel, these studies will influence the recipients' response. (Fukuda, 1992:186)

We should think about the needs of the community and carefully prepare channels which draw unreached people into the local church. If the members understand the methods that the church is going to use, they can minister effectively within their mission field.

As well as this, ministers should listen to their members concerning mission strategy. Lay church members know about the unchurched better than ministers. If ministers just set out their policies for mission strategy to their members and do not ask them about their ideas, they may lose their effectiveness. If, however, ministers believe and trust that their members are good co-workers, they will hear beneficial feedback from the laity about their proposed strategies.

5.4.5 Expectation

The most essential dimension in mission should be the work of the Holy Spirit. We must expect the Holy Spirit to work in every aspect of our mission process. There seem to be two realms in which we presume the Spirit works: the outer part and the inner part of every human being.

Needless to say, the visible work of the Spirit makes a forceful impression even on unbelievers. "Pentecostals believe that the coming of the Spirit brings an ability to do 'signs and wonders' in the name of Jesus Christ to accompany and authenticate the gospel message." (Anderson, 2005) As indicated, if the unchurched experience the work of the Holy Spirit, they will know that the Gospel that we present is not just philosophical knowledge but living truth.

At the same time, we should believe that the Holy Spirit can touch not only the body but also the human mind and heart. Many Japanese are nursing serious problems in their hearts. There are over 30,000 Japanese who commit suicide a year.[4] We must expect the Spirit to heal people inwardly. We Pentecostals should always pray for the work of the Spirit, not only in the Sunday worship but also in small group activities. Chan (2000) states, "Prayer for healing of the body, mind, and spirit must be a regular part of the Pentecostal church's *liturgical* life." (Emphasis in original.)

If we do not expect the Holy Spirit to work effectively and merely rely upon our mission strategy, we will see nothing. "We have to remember that we do not do the mission, but we

---

[4]See, e.g., The Metropolitan Police Department, *Progress of the Number of Suicides,* http://www.t-pec.co.jp/mental/2002-08-4.htm, August 30, 2005.

have been graciously invited to be partners of God in laboring for his kingdom." (Ma, 2004)

Chapter 6

Concluding Remarks

Why do Japanese reject the Gospel? Is it because they hate Christianity? Do they think that the Gospel has nothing to do with their lives? Are they satisfied with and committed to the teachings of Buddhism or Shinto? Many non-Christians probably do not think so. But if we are seriously looking for the key to unlock a great spiritual awakening in Japan, we have to make a serious effort to understand Japanese religious thought and the Japanese mindset, and find a way of presenting the Gospel that meshes with Japanese thinking.

As mentioned in chapter two, Japanese accept or understand religious truth not by intellectual study but by active participation in ritual. Unless they participate in and experience something, they will never believe in religious truth. Experience is very important for them. What is more, we must not overlook the fact that Japanese cannot separate believing religious truth from belonging to a community. For Japanese, religion (Shinto and Buddhism) has been the tie that has formed the village community and the household. Japanese respect that to which they belong, rather than what they believe. Finally, in their mindset, it is difficult for Japanese to grant that there is an Absolute God who rules everything.

The most important characteristic of the Japanese mindset is its group orientation. Japanese people find their value by playing a significant part in the group to which they belong. Everything is decided within the context of a group. For ordinary Japanese, to become a Christian may mean leaving their community, their household or their village. Without providing a community to which they can belong, it is difficult for Japanese to join a Christian circle.

In the 16th century, Catholic missionaries came to Japan for evangelism, and later, in the 19th century, Protestant missionaries also came to Japan and tried to evangelize the Japanese people. Christianity has had a great influence on Japanese society as a result of their fervent efforts. Even now, Christianity continues to have a great impact on many aspects of Japanese life, such as education (more than 10% of new colleges and universities are Christian), (Furuya, 2003:31) medical services and social services. Unfortunately, however, the number of the converts has not been as much as has been expected. In a word, the vast majority of Japanese people cannot see a connection between their lives and the Christian church.

I conclude that one of the biggest reasons why Christianity does not penetrate the Japanese mind is that the conventional approach of the Christian mission does not seem to fit the religious mindset of ordinary Japanese, in that we have been trying to force the Japanese to accept the absoluteness of God as the first step within an intellectual approach to evangelism.

The intellectual approach is not the way that the Japanese accept religious truth. As well as this, we have also tried to evangelize the people as individuals. To be sure, faith is a personal decision, but it is difficult for Japanese people to make a decision about religion as a personal resolution, since Japanese have never had any experience of choosing a religion during their lifetime. Almost all Japanese have acquired their religion (Buddhism and Shintoism) as a family birthright rather than as a personal decision, and they grow up participating in ritual ceremonies such as *Omiya Mairi* (the visitation of a newborn baby to a Shinto shrine) and *Shichi Go San* (the festival day for children aged seven, five, and three). It is this ritual participation which gives Japanese people the sense that they belong to a household and a local community.

In other words, Japanese receive religious reality by joining a community, experiencing religious episodes, and then finding religious truth, and yet, the mission approach that we have been using thus far does not seem to suit the Japanese mind. I express the conventional mission approach as follows:

To hear $\rightarrow$ To understand $\rightarrow$ To believe

The conventional mission approach focuses on making the people hear the Gospel and understand that Jesus Christ is the truth, before leading them into believing. Then, if they believe, they become a member of a church. In a word, belonging comes last. This is the typical intellectual and individualistic approach, and does not fit with the Japanese mindset.

I would like to suggest a paradigm shift of evangelism, expressed as follows;

To belong to → To experience → To believe

I believe that the spiritual community has the power to attract lost people. We should accept people before making them decide whether they believe or not. People are seeking love. We see a lot of breakdown within human relationships in Japanese society—between parents and children in family, husbands and wives in marriage, teachers and students in school; there is much distrust in our society. I believe that there are many problems that only the Church can solve. We Christian churches have to open our eyes to the wounds of the people and offer cures through specific action.

We need to first present a community filled with true love. The Bible tells us, "Love comes from God." (1 John 4:7). We have the love that people are looking for. If we can meet their physical and mental needs with love from God, we can open their hearts. If people realize that the true love that they are seeking is found within the Christian community, they will want to join us and will eventually open their hearts to the Good News. If they can see and touch what God is doing through Christian fellowship, they will come to understand that they need Jesus Christ as their Saviour.

We need to be presenting God as the God who created everything, even Japan, and not as the God whom the Western missionaries brought from their countries. As St. Paul explained to the people of Athens,

> For as I was passing through and considering the objects of your worship, I even found an altar with this inscription: TO THE UNKNOWN

82

GOD. Therefore, the One whom you worship without knowing, Him I proclaim to you:... (Acts 17:23 NKJ)

The God of Christianity is the "unknown god" that Japanese have been seeking since they were created.

I believe that there is an essential key Scripture in the Bible for Pentecostal mission in Japan. Chapter 2 of the book of Acts describes the first Christian community.

And they continued steadfastly in the apostles' doctrine and fellowship, in the breaking of bread, and in prayers. Then fear came upon every soul, and many wonders and signs were done through the apostles. Now all who believed were together, and had all things in common, and sold their possessions and goods, and divided them among all, as anyone had need. So continuing daily with one accord in the temple, and breaking bread from house to house, they ate their food with gladness and simplicity of heart, praising God and having favour with all the people. And the Lord added to the church daily those who were being saved. (Acts 2:42-47 NKJ)

The first Christians eagerly learned the Word of God and prayed together (verse 42). There were signs and wonders within the Christian fellowship (verse 43). Their needs were met through each other (verses 44-5). They had joy (verse 46). I especially would like to stress that they had favour with people who were outside the Christian community, and that daily people were being saved (47). We can say that the first Christian community was successful in attracting people who were outside the Church.

I believe that the Japanese Pentecostals should notice the first Christian community described in Acts 2:42-47 as well as in Acts 2:1-4. The Spirit-filled community drew people who did not know who Jesus was. These people were accepted by the Christian fellowship, their needs were met, and they felt the love of God. They experienced the work of the Holy Spirit and realized the truth that Jesus was the Lord. The key principle was the Holy Spirit. The first Christians expected the Spirit to work freely. They never approached lost people by means of an intellectual method. In the same way, this principle should work even in Japan.

We must think how we can meet the needs of lost people. Our focus should be specific and practical. Our strategies may end up looking new and unique and may not be the traditional church style, but we must not fear criticism from other Christians. We have to have the mindset that we are sent by God to serve the people of the local community.

We Japanese have to theologize as Asians and as Japanese. To contextualize the Christian church into our society, we should avoid both accepting Western theology uncritically, and, equally, we should avoid rejecting Japanese tradition and culture uncritically. We should continuously seek to develop our own theology to fit the Japanese context and mind. Above all, we have to develop a theology dealing with ancestor worship which escapes from syncreticism. We also should develop a theology treating Pentecostal pneumatology in dialogue with Japanese spirituality.

Finally, the most important point is to be a spiritual community. The Japanese Church should break free from its clergy-centered mindset. While the first Christians respected the authority of the apostles, they ministered voluntarily and served together even in their own houses. The Pentecostal church should be a church in which every believer can and does exercise their own gifts. The ministers have to cultivate their members and delegate ministry tasks to their members. If we can build a real, Spirit-filled Church like the first Christian fellowship described in the book of Acts, we can turn the Pentecostal movement into a grass roots movement in Japan.

I believe that God loves Japan and that only Jesus can save this country. When we trust only Him and seek to be a Spirit-filled church, we can reach people of every social level. I do not believe it is unrealistic to seek for revival in Japan. I pray that we will see a great spiritual awakening in Japan, and that the Japanese church can have great impact all over the world for the sake of His Kingdom.

Bibliography

Titles given in square brackets are the author's translation of Japanese titles.

Ama, T. (1999). *Nihonjin wa Naze Mu-Shukyo Nanoka [Why Do Japanese Have no Religion]*, Japan: Chikuma Shobo.

Anderson, A. (2005). Towards a pentecostal missiology for the majority world, *Asian Journal of Pentecostal Studies* 8(1).

Benedict, R. (1967). *The Chrysanthemum and the Sword: Patterns of Japanese Culture (Cleveland*, New York: Word Books.

Boyle, T. D. (1986). *Communicating the Gospel in Japanese Cultural Terms: Practical Experiments at the Shintoku Kyodan Church*, PhD thesis, Fuller Theological Seminary.

Chan, S. (2000). *Pentecostal Theology and the Christian Spiritual Tradition*, Sheffield: Sheffield Academic Press.

Davis, M. B. (ed.) (1992). *Japan*, Insight Guides, Singapore: APA Publications (HK).

Doi, H. (1971). *Amae no Kozo [The Structure of "Amae"]*, Tokyo: Kobundo.

Drummond, R. (1971). *A History of Christianity in Japan*, New York: William B. Eerdmans.

Ebisawa, A. and Saburo, O. (1970). *Nihon Kirisutokyoshi [A History of Japanese Christianity]*, Japan: Nihon Kirisutoky-odan Shuppankyoku.

Eibun Nihon Daijiten [English-Japanese Dictionary] (ed.) (1996). *Keys to the Japanese Heart and Soul*, Japan: Kodansha.

Fujita, N. S. (1991). *Japan's Encounter with Christianity: the Catholic mission in pre-modern Japan*, New York: Paulist Press.

Fukuda, M. (1992). *Developing A Contextualized Church As A Bridge To Christianity in Japan*, PhD thesis, Pasadena, Fuller Theological Seminary.

Fukuda, M. (2001). Sermon topics contextualized for japan, *Journal of Asian Mission* 3(1).

Fukuda, M. (ed.) (2002). *Senkyo-Gaku Riidingusu Nihon Bunka to Kirisutokyo [Missiological Readings: Japanese Culture and Christianity]*, Japan: RAC Network.

Furuya, Y. (2003). *Nihon no Kirisutokyo [Christianity in Japan]*, Tokyo: Kyobunkwan.

Goto, M. (1959). *Dendo no Riron to Jissai [Evangelism Theory and Practice]*, Tokyo: Inochi no Kotoba.

Goto, M. (2002). Nihon Senkyo-Gaku ga Toriatsukaubeki Han-i N itsuite [About the Range That the Japanese Missiology Should Deal With], *in* M. Fukuda (ed.), *Senkyo-Gaku Riidingusu Nihon Bunka to Kirisutokyo [Missiological Readings: Japanese Culture and Christianity]*, Japan: RAC Network.

Hamaguchi, E. (1982). *Kanjin Shugino Shakai Nippon [The Society of "Kanjin" Japan]*, Japan: Toyo Keizai Shinposha.

Hiyane, A. (1949). *Nihon Kirisutokyo Shi [The History of Christianity in Japan]*, Tokyo: Kyobunkwan.

Holiness Band Showa Kirisutokyo Danatsushi Kankokai (1983). *Horinesu Bando no Kiseki Ribaibaru to Kirisutokyo Dan-atsu [The Locus of the Holiness Band: Revival and Persecution]*, Tokyo: Holiness Band Showa Kirisutokyo Danatsushi Kankokai.

Holiness Conference North America (2003). Facts About the Holiness Conference, http://www.omsholiness.org/info/download/facts.pdf.

Ishii, K. (1997). *Gendai Nihonjin no Shukyo [Today's Japanese Religion]*, Japan: Shinyosha.

Kaneda, R. (1996). *Showa Nihon Kirisutokyoshi [The History of the Church of Christ in Japan in Showa Era: Under the Emperor System & the Fifty Years War]*, Tokyo: Shinkyo Shuppan.

Karkkainen, V. M. (2002). Missiology: Pentecostal and charismatic, *The New International Dictionary of Pentecostal and Charismatic Movements*, Grand Rapids: Zondervan.

Kato, H. (1992). Nihon no Kamigami [Popular Deities of Japan], *in* Corporate Secretariat Division, Nippon Steel Corporation (ed.), *Nihon no Kokoro: Bunka to Dento [Inside the Japanese: Culture and Tradition]*, Japan: Maruzen.

Katsumoto, M. (1990). *Nihon no Shukyo Gyoji ni Dou Taiou Suruka [How Do we Deal with Japanese Religious Events?]*, Tokyo: Inochi no Kotoba.

Kondo, K. (2002). *Dendo no Shingaku: 21-Seiki Kirisutokyo Dendo no Tameni [Theology of Evangelization For 21st Century Mission]*, Tokyo: Kyobunkwan.

Kondo, K. (2004). *Dendo Suru Kyokaino Keisei Naze, Naniwo Ikani Dendo Suruka [The Formation of Church That Evangelizes: Why, What, How to Evangelize]*, Tokyo: Kyobunkwan.

Kudo, H. (1965). Bakkusuton [Buxton], *in* A. Hiyane (ed.), *Shi Kirisutokyo Jiten [The New Dictionary of Christianity]*, Tokyo: Inochi no Kotoba.

Kurisuchan Shimbun (2003). *Kurisuchan Joho Bukku 2003 [Christian Data Book 2003]*, Japan: Inochi no Kotoba.

Kurisuchan Shimbun [The Christian Newspaper] (2001). Kyokai de furii sukuuru [free school at the church].

Ma, J. (2004). Church Planting: Strategy for Mission among Pentecostals, *Journal of Asian Mission* 6(2).

Mandai, E. (2000). 21 Seiki no Pentekosute-Karisuma-undo to Nihon no Senkyo [The Pentecostal/Charismatic Movement and the Mission in Japan in the 21st Century], *Signs: A Journal for the Pentecostal-Charismatic Movement in Today's Japan* (4).

Ministry of Health and Welfare (2005). White paper: The prospect of aging society, http://www8.cao.go.jp/kourei/whitepaper/w-2004/zenbun/html/G1110000.html.

Mullins, M. R. (1998). *Christianity Made in Japan: A Study of Indigenous Movements*, Honolulu: U of Hawaii Press.

Nagasawa, M. (2002). Religious truth, *Journal of Asian Mission* 4(1).

Nakamura, S. (2003). *Nihon ni Okeru Fukuinha no Rekishi Mou Hitotsu no Nihon Kirisutokyoshi [The History of the Evangelicals in Japan: Other History of Japanese Christianity]*, Tokyo: Inochi no Kotoba.

Nakamura, T. (1965). The History of Japanese Mission, *in* A. Hiyane (ed.), *Shi Kirisutokyo Jiten [The New Dictionary of Christianity]*, Tokyo: Inochi no Kotoba.

Nakane, C. (1972). *Human Relations in Japan: Summary Translation of "Tateshakai no Ningen Kankei" (Personal Relations in a Vertical Society)*, Japan: Ministry of Foreign Affairs.

Nicolas, A. (2003). Daini Bachikan Kokaigi Igo no Nihon-shakai to Senkyo [Japanese Society and Mission After the Second Vatican Council], *in* C. Cavagna and A. Nicolas (eds), *Nihon no Kyokai no Senkyo no Hikari to Kage [The Light and Shadow of the Mission of Japanese Church]*, Japan: St. Paul.

Nihon Assenburiizu obu Goddo Kyodan (1989). *Oncho no Kiseki*, Tokyo: Shinri no Honoo.

Nihon Assenburiizu obu Goddo Kyodan Rekishi Hensan Iinkai (1999). *Mikotoba ni Tachi, Mitama ni Michibikarete [Standing On the Word and Guided by the Spirit: The 50 Years History Since the Founding]*, Tokyo: Nihon Assenburiizu obu Goddo Kyodan.

Ogata, M. B. (1997). *Nikkan Kyokai Seicho Hikaku Bunka to Kirisutkyoshi [The Comparison of Japanese and Korean Church Growth: Culture and History of Christianity]*, Japan: Hope Shuppan.

Osumi, K. (1992). Nihon ni okeru Shukyo: Shinto-Bukkyo no Seiritu to Heiritu [Religion in Japan: The Interweaving of Shinto and Buddhism], *in* Corporate Secretariat Division, Nippon Steel Corporation (ed.), *Nihon no Kokoro: Bunka to Dento [Inside the Japanese: Culture and Tradition]*, Japan: Maruzen.

Oyama, R. (1995). *Nihonjin to Kirisutokyo no Juyo [Japanese and the Acceptance of Christianity]*, Japan: Yogunsha.

Pinnock, C. H. (1996). *Flame of Love: A Theology of the Holy Spirit*, Downers Grove: InterVarsity Press.

Reischauer, E. O. (1972). *The Japanese*, North Clarendon: Charles Tuttle.

Ribaibaru Shimbun [The Revival Times] (2003a). Jogosiki-dendo de Shintensuru Kaitakudendo [The Church Planting Developed by the Evangelism of the Funnel Style].

Ribaibaru Shimbun [The Revival Times] (2003b). Josei Minisutorii STAND Sutaato [Women's Ministry STAND Starts].

Saito, M. (1981). *Kirisutokyo no Rekishi [The History of Christianity]*, Tokyo: Shinkyo Shuppan.

Sakurai, K. (2002). *Ikyo Sekai no Kirisutokyo [Christianity in the Pagan World]*, Japan: Inochi no Kotoba.

Senoo, M. (2001). Nihon Niokeru Junfukuinkyokai no Ayumi to Tenbo [The History and the Vista of Full Gospel Church in Japan Mission], *Signs: A Journal for the Pentecostal-Charismatic Movement in Today's Japan* (5).

Shew, P. (2002). A forgotten history: Correcting the historical record of the roots of Pentecostalism in Japan1, *Asian Journal of Pentecostal Studies* 5(1): 23–49.

Shew, P. T. (2003). *History of the Early Pentecostal Movement in Japan: The Roots and Development of the Pre-War Pentecostal Movement in Japan*, PhD thesis, Pasadena, Fuller Theological Seminary.

Shinsho Kirisuto Kyokai (2002). *Kamini Meshiastumerarete: Kendo 75 Shunen Kinenshi [Called by God: Memorial Book of 75 Anniversary]*, Japan: Assemblies of God Church.

Shiono, K. (1997). *Nihon Kirisutokyoshi wo Yomu [Reading a History of Japanese Christianity]*, Tokyo: Shinkyo Shuppan.

Smith, R. J. (1974). *Ancestor Worship in Contemporary Japan*, Stanford: Stanford University Press.

Soboku na Gimon Tankyukai [Simple Questions Research Association] (ed.) (1998). *Eigo de Hanasu Zatsugaku Nippon [Japan Trivia]*, Japan: Kodansha.

Suzuki, M. (2001a). A New Look at the Pre-War History of the Japan Assemblies of God, *Asian Journal of Pentecostal Studies* 4(2).

Suzuki, N. (2001b). *Nihon Kirisutokyoshi Monogatari [Story of Japanese Christianity History]*, Tokyo: Kyobunkwan.

Takaguchi, K. (2002). *Rekishini Hito Ari, Rekishini Kami Ari: Yumiyama Sensei no Ashiato [There Are Men in History, There Is God in History: The Footsteps of Yumiyama]*, Tokyo: Fukuin Shuppansha.

Yoshiyama, H. (2001). 21-seiki ni kitaisuru nihon no seirei undo [the holy spirit movement in 21th century], *Signs: A Journal for the Pentecostal-Charismatic Movement in Today's Japan* .

Yuasa, Y. (1999). *Nihonjin no Shukyo Ishiki [Japanese Religious Thinking]*, Japan: Kodansha.

Yumiyama, K. (1977). *Yumiyama Kiyoma Sekkyo Shu Vol. 1 [The Collection of the Sermons of Kiyoma Yumiyama]*, Tokyo: Nihon Assenburiizu obu Goddo Kyodan.

Lightning Source UK Ltd.
Milton Keynes UK
UKHW020001250519
343286UK00008B/1025/P